The Double Houdini

Based on a true story: Any resemblance to actual persons, living or dead, may be no more than coincidence. (Tudor Rickards, in *The Double Houdini*)

It was a wrong number that started it, the telephone ringing in the dead of the night and asking for someone. Much later, when he was able to think about the things that had happened to him, he would conclude that nothing was real except chance.
(Paul Auster, in *The New York Trilogy*)

Dr Auster, who lives in Brookyn, New York, is the best-selling author of *The Invention of Solitude*, and *The New York Trilogy*, an award-winning series of literary detective stories in which the author appears in a baffling way. (Tudor Rickards, in *The Double Houdini*)

~~Any resemblance to actual persons, living or dead, is purely coincidental~~ The disclaimer has a neat line through it. A message she failed to notice when she opened the book. There is no mistaking the resemblance to her. She is a key character, a main player.
(Renee Knight, in *Disclaimer*)

Disclaimer

 It draws on and modifies reports posted on web-sites of clubs in the Stockport Chess League, and particularly from the East Cheshire club.

The basic idea of survival against the odds does draw on the battles to avoid relegation at East Cheshire in the season 2015-6. However, the fictional East Cheadle club and its characters exist in an imaginary world, and any resemblance to real people should be taken as coincidental.

Acknowledgements

Where to begin? With Susan, who, as ever, continues to give substantial support both to my weird working hours at my laptop and to our finances at the end of each month.

Members of my real-life chess club provided countless suggestions as well as permission to draw on accounts of matches which I have captured and reproduced for my fictional purposes.

A special thanks to the real-life Phil, Paul, Ian, Keith, Jim, Bill, Edwin, Keven, Myles and a plurality of Daves, Steves, Geoffs, and others who ideas I may have taken thoughtlessly and *en passant*.

Similar kindnesses were received from members of other real-life chess clubs and league officials. Without these, I could never have made progress towards completing the book. Reg, Jill, Mike, Peter, you know who you are.

Professor Syd Howell found time to test the Latin and Greek sources of the myth of Caissa, patron saint of Chess.

David Shaw and Hans Mock, chess-playing mentors at the Northern Tennis Club Didsbury, offered invaluable professional insights.

GM Jon Speelman offered his much appreciated encouragement after reading an early draft.

Inevitably, if I have misunderstood information I received, I can only plead the well-worn excuse that my imagination may have distorted material I have imported from a world outside these pages.

Preface

Some years ago I lay in a bed in a large regional hospital, recovering from surgery. This is a verifiable fact.

But when I tried to record accurately what was happening to me, I arrived at the same conclusion many others have reached over the years, namely that truth is a slippery commodity.

I postponed writing the hospital documentary, and began concentrating on other stories I knew something about. The theme running through these books is a comparison between behaviours and beliefs of top achievers and more modest practitioners. In *Mourinho Matters* I compared the ultimate charismatic Jose Mourinho with Sunday park-team players and their parents. In *Tennis Matters*, and *Tennis Tensions* I drew on my own hapless club efforts and looked for evidence that I shared at least some of the emotions and aspirations of my tennis heroes past and present.

The Double Houdini is again based on a true story. It is derived from my experiences in a community of which I am part, which is to be found deep in the sleepy shires of East Cheshire. The community-based club has been given the fictional name of the East Cheadle Chess Club.

That being said, my intention has been to imagine not report, to bring characters to life, as an imagined and yet realistic case study.

The closest literary example I can think of is the approach taken in The *New York Trilogy* by Paul Auster, who inserts himself as a character and an author into his brilliant work drawing attention to those boundaries between fact and fiction.

Only later did the uncomfortable thought occur to me that I might also have been influenced by the approach towards fictionalizing real life pioneered by Truman Capote, especially in his great work, *In Cold Blood*, a grimmer account of real-life murders than you will find in *The Double Houdini*, although there is plenty of blood spilled over the chess board in these pages.

The book is about leadership, community, personal crises and struggles against the odds that would have tested the escapologist Harry Houdini. For non-chess players I suggest you accept the mentions of chess terms. These are mostly openings with exotic names such as *The Sicilian Dragon*, *The Kings Indian Defence*, *The Leningrad Dutch*, and *The Queen's Gambit*. Susan, who doesn't play chess, encouraged me to retain them, saying they did not get in the way of the story, and added a touch of reality to it.

There are also mentions of *time controls*, a source of tension in serious games since the game was speeded up with hourglasses in the nineteenth century. The ingenious *Fischer Time Control* invented by the great World Champion Bobby Fischer continues the process. This requires electronic clocks which add a pre-agreed increment of time after each move played.

T.R., 'East Cheadle', 2016

A Surfeit of Daves and a Multiplicity of Michaels

In writing The Double Houdini, I found myself facing a problem which I never solved to my complete satisfaction. It might be described as a surfeit of Daves. Whenever I encountered it, I was reminded of a distant time in a different place, and the tale of the multiple Michaels.

In an earlier profession I was once working for a well-known producer of a much-loved and imbibed product which I will cunningly disguise as *McGuinness*.

My partner Susan and I found ourselves in a beautiful location to the South of Dublin. A group of elite purveyors of liquid hope had been gathered together to determine in what ways they might be able to add value to their already wondrous product.

We were there to help the new ideas ferment, so to speak. We were, as the Germans put it, *Fachpromotors*, or as the Americans say *Idea Facilitators*. We met up with eighteen sales and marketing managers who had been arranged into three teams.

The room was the sort about which business trainers dream. Spacious, clean, elegant seating around three walnut dining-tables now converted for some serious mind work with adequate supplies of pencils, pads, and mints.

Not unlike our own Chess league today, women were somewhat in a minority. They were represented by

Aisling, one eighteenth of the group, who was treated by the others as some form of Celtic royalty. This might have been helped by her likeness to Galadriel in Lord of the Rings, and an emerald green gleam in her eyes. Aisling today could have understudied for the warrior queen in *Game of Thrones*.

I was struck by the physical scale of most of the participants. Fortunately, they brought with them the gentle joviality of a group of rugby forwards settling down to a good session of *craic* after an enjoyable afternoon of pummelling in the scrum.

These training gigs start with *The Naming of Names*. "Let's stick to first names", I said.

Mischievous fate or mischievous Michaels had co-located five of the six Michaels in the room around one table. One the hugest of the huge participants spoke up, smiling in a guileless way.

"I'm Michael. From up the road there, in Blackrock".

He eased himself back, threatening damage to his chair, and looked across at the even larger fellow next to him, who had an even wider smile and wider shoulders. Someone had rearranged his nose and turned his left ear into a squash plant. "I'm Michael, from Waterford".

As successive Michaels offered up their identical moniker, the amusement level in the room rose. On the table at the back, one of the participants was roaring encouragement, tears of laughter running down his ruddy features.

A disturbing thought struck me. Were they all called Michael, or were they all taking the Mickey Bliss? I decided against risking offense by checking whether the metaphoric urine was being extracted. Michael of the rearranged ear handed over to the giant to his right.

"My name, would you know it now? It's Michael. You'd be right, there." He bellowed loudly enough to rise the tide in the Liffey. Now the whole mood was one of boisterous good humour "I'm the one from Kilkenny".

Was I dreaming this? Was I expected to laugh, or give the appearance of the bemused traveller?

The next man in turn was as small as his teammates were ginormous. Obviously the team's jockey-sized hooker. "So where are you from, Michael?"

The table almost collapsed under the weight of mirth. They might have shouted *gottcha* or its Gaelic equivalent.

"Jaysis, no. I'm not one of those Michael fellows, sure look it. I'm your Brendon now, from Limerick."

Checkmate. Susan and I joined in the laughter.

We had a whale of a time for two days after that. And we worked out a simple way of distinguishing the Michaels. There was Blackrock Michael, Waterford Michael, Kilkenny Michael, and Macgillycuddy Michael. We had had our first encounter of the problem of too many people with the same name in a social group.

Which brings us nicely to the naming problem which haunts these pages. East Cheadle has three registered players each blessed with the ancient and honourable name David, or, in its affectionate informal form, Dave. The scope for confusion is obvious. In one match, we played another team with two Daves. And it turned out that the first two boards had the four Daves locked in combat.

Why does this matter? Because as an author you try to avoid unintended confusion. Giving characters the same name doesn't work. Think *Sherlock Holmes* and *Sherlock Watson*. Or what if a great chess match was played between *Magnus Carlsen* and *Magnus Anand*; or *Bobby Fischer* and *Bobby Spassky*.

For better or worse, I adapted the McGuinness naming-strategy in these pages for differentiating the Daves, Geoffs and Mikes I knew in real-life.

It is not unlike the time-honoured approach found in Wales, where it is deployed to distinguish the multiple Jones found in any township as Jones the baker, Jones the Papers, Jones from Cwm Lane, Jones the singer, and so on.

New Members Start Here

From: T.R.
To: New Club Members

September 2015

Welcome to East Cheadle Chess Club, home of the world's first cryogenic training facilities; extensive car parking (four spaces behind the main hall, plus access to the nearby Health Centre); good neighbours (quiet snooker players in upstairs room); unisex toilets; kitchen area; tethering points for parents, carers and guide dogs.

I write as unofficial chronicler of the club. From time to time you will be getting news bulletins from myself and other contributors (who mostly wish to remain anonymous). These complement the more reliable and believable official messages to be found on the club website.

We at East Cheadle pride ourselves in the warm welcome given to players of all strengths, from super heavyweight to flyweight categories.

The season just ended saw remarkable successes in all league and cup competitions. In League matches, our teams toyed with the competition, fooling them into believing we were heading for relegation, before our last-minute rescue acts which are known as our Houdini escapes.

In the cup competitions we were just as successful, rarely defaulting, or being disqualified for setting the clocks to the incorrect time format.

Our social evenings are well frequented, both for the ten-minute chess competition, prizes, and the food and drink provided by the members.

As a club, we are still under-represented by grandmasters, players for our junior team, females, and ethnic minorities, including immigrants from across the Welsh border.

One misconception concerns the setting-up of the tables, chess boards, clocks, and score sheets on club nights: Nowhere in the club rules is it said that these tasks are only to be carried out by the elders of the club.

I myself have hung back for several years, so that our President Geoff (referred to affectionately as the *Dalai Lama*), and our equally esteemed Secretary David (*Dave the Power*) can carry out these sacramental duties. Both assure me that members barely eligible for a winter fuel allowance may also play a part on request.

The *Unfolding of the Tables* is also of great significance, and much humour is to be gained if a novice is unable to release a pair of table legs, and in attempting to do so receives a painful tweak of the fingers.

Another event not to be missed is the *Annual General Meeting*. There is always great competition at the AGM to avoid the most onerous committee posts on offer. I am in no position to urge others to volunteer, as I have repeatedly avoided doing so myself for personal reasons.

However, it does seem that the few are taking the greatest share of the social burdens on behalf of the rest of us.

Major Max

Most members of East Cheadle are too young to remember Major Max McIntyre. He helped found the club, and was a prominent member during the battle for secession which resulted in the formation of East Cheadle and West Cheadle.

After the split, West Cheadle flourished briefly and now plays in the *Mid Cheshire and Merseyside league* under its new name The *Post Modernists.*

Cheadle first met as *The Cheadle Hulme British Legion Club.* Max joined as a schoolboy and remembers the distinguished club secretary Mr Clive Sinclair, (not the famous inventor) who was active in the formation of a local league in the 1950s. Other founding clubs were Stockport, Hyde, Marple Bridge, Macclesfield, North West Car Road Company, and Wilmslow.

Over the years, Major Max became a stalwart of the club, occupying the offices of treasurer, secretary, and eventually President. He was among the strongest players in the league, and also played for the Cheshire county team.

He is no longer an active player, but remains involved in the club through his friend, and now president, The Dalai Lama.

Both the Major and the Dalai Lama have resisted the rise of new-fangled ways of communicating. They exchange notes in beautifully written script. Messages of general interest are sometimes passed on to the other members by the current secretary (at the time of writing,

Dave the Power, one of the most diligent and energetic in the club's history).

At the start of the 2015-16 season, Major Max produced one of his announcements, which was passed on to the membership by the Secretary, who received it from the President

From: Major Max
To: All members

I note from the minutes of the last general meeting that various efforts are being made to recruit new members. Whilst such initiatives are to be applauded, I would like to point out that the major source of new members for a considerable time has been the very visible sign on the front of our premises on Church Road.

The sign was erected by Roy Huddleston, a player I remember from my playing time, when he rarely missed a club-night. The sign bears his home telephone number and I know he follows up all enquiries and then meets and greets them. Such a welcome is a good recruiting officer. I would like a formal acknowledgement to be made of Roy's years of service as he approaches his eightieth birthday.

This brings me to another matter I would like to draw to your attention. In the past, it was customary for members to attend in a lounge suit and wearing a single or double breasted waist coat, and tie. I favoured a regimental tie, Windsor-knotted. For others it was a chance to show school or varsity colours. Dr Stacks until his passing, retained the correctly tied bow-tie he always wore in his surgery on Emms Lane.

The President tells me that younger members are favouring what is known as *smart casual* wear. I find the expression an oxymoron. I realise that times are changing and even he attends club nights in what looks to me like an arctic foraging jacket. If indeed this is now acceptable, we may need to discuss a dress code for members.

I am encouraged to learn that most of our club officials are still supporters of the more traditional style of dress. All is not completely lost. *Non est totum perditum.*

Relegation Battles are behind us

September 2015

From the Minutes of the AGM
East Cheadle Chess Club
Memorial Hall
Cheadle

Extract from Phil's report as First Team Captain

An excellent year for the first team, with a great finish which secured promotion of the first team to division one of the league after a tie-break on games won.

As you know, we have yo-yoed up and down several times over the years. We will be even more out-graded in the first division, but with the contributions from our new members Steve and Geoff, we are in a great position to avoid being called the *Yo-yo Boys* again.

It means we will not have to worry with a relegation battle and having to rely on a win over our own B team for survival.

Sadly, the A team is still likely to be weakened by the periods when two or three key players become unavailable for selection.

Extract from Paul's report as Second Team Captain

Another tough year, when we battled through for survival in division two. The half point gained in one of our encounters with the first team was to prove vital in the end. The good form shown by Bill who achieved a plus score in league games, also helped save our bacon.

The new members playing for the first team mean that we will be able to borrow one or two much-needed players in times of shortage. As a result, I believe that our relegation battles are also now behind us.

Unlike the first team, we have only one member with luxury second-homes in exotic locations, although last-minute withdrawals for more local domestic pressures have contributed to some of our losses.

Extract from Myles' report as Third Team Captain

The newly-formed third team is feeling its way into competitive chess. As a relatively new member of East Cheadle, I am honoured to be given the chance to take on the onerous duties as its captain which I will share with Edwin.

It is too early yet to make predictions about our progress against more experienced teams. We have our targets which are top secret and locked away in a secure place. I can say that we also have a few surprises in store for our opponents.

Extract from Keith's report as Limit League Captain

The new Limit League competition is so named as there are limits to the grades of players in it. No one with a grade above 120 is permitted to play.

In this first season to our surprise we won the league. The dedication and enthusiasm of all the members taking part in the matches both home and away is testament to our enjoyment as well as our over the board successes. I am happy to report that we fielded a full team without defaulting a board throughout the season.

I wish to thank all the team players who took part in achieving such a successful season. This year we expect it to be tougher, but we will fight for our title.

Our new slogan is: *The Sky is the Limit.*

Extract from The Dalai Lama's Report

As President, I am grateful to all our officials and other members who contributed so much, not just in our league games but the numerous onerous tasks including getting the hall ready for matches.

I want to thank them for their dedication to what must sometimes have seemed a hopeless cause.

It is good news to learn that our darkest days are over.

It is invidious to single out one team, but the magnificent results achieved by the Limit League team deserves special mention.

A special thanks goes to Keith as captain. We take a special pride in the formation of this league, and we have worked hard to make it happen.

I for one am pleased that my score remains at a level that will enable me to play again in the Limit League.

I look forward to our next AGM, after what we all believe will be our most successful season for some years.

It is a great pleasure to learn we have turned the corner, and that our annual battles to avoid relegation are things of the past.

Next week, your representatives will be attending the league meeting at Stockport to arrange fixtures for each of the teams for next season.

You will be hearing what has been arranged from the club secretary, and then from the captain who will be making your team selections.

The league has discontinued the practice of producing a league handbook, but all information can now be found on our noticeboard, and through the League website.

Phil's First Team Fighters

The AGM proceeded as it usually does. I found myself jotting down some notes for a new monograph on the back of the financial statement provided us. I was far from convinced that chess would be a subject likely to attract a large readership. The market is stuffed full of books by the great players in the game.

But as the meeting went on (and on) I experienced that mysterious sense of anticipation that maybe I was witnessing the start of a story that would be worth following. It was not unlike the feeling I had about the story developing as Chelsea started their football season so badly in the early months of the 2015-16 season.

As Phil mentioned in his report, the first team at East Cheadle is made up of stubborn street-fighters. On their day, they can surprise the strongest opposition.

I began compiling a dossier of my fellow members, starting with the elite forces of the club under Phil's command:

Cap'n Phil

Carries the burdens of first-team leadership valiantly and uncomplainingly, even when his first selection is thwarted by trivial excuses such as key members being out of the country, recovering from hip surgery, working night shifts, or more unconvincing explanations for unavailability.

He displays rare tea-cupping ability (*thinking clearly under pressure*) in matches. Phil also does wonders at our regular social quick-play competitions, arranging the rounds thanks to his astonishing IT skills, and even then often finishing in the top three, taking away one of the bottles of wine provided by the members.

John Reed-Warbler (Greater Crested)

Long-time top board, fighting regular battles against the strongest players of other clubs, often defying the predictions of the ELO ranking system to pull off an astonishing victory.

A brilliant teacher who gives outstanding talks about chess to our other members from time to time. He actually was a teacher, and probably a brilliant one before he decided to trade up to a different life-style.

Unfortunately for us, this means he is unavoidably unavailable for selection for long periods. For some unaccountable reason he now prefers photographing exotic birds of African safaris, or playing high-level chess in the South of France rather than in various parts of Stockport and its surrounding bandit regions.

Steve Tarantula

One of our new hopes for taking the top-board burden away from John. Named after his deadly attacks, from which few opponents recover. Like John Reed-Warbler, plays in strong international events from which we have to entice him back to over-winter in Northern England.

Geoff Bristle

Another new recruit who is strengthening the first team's survival prospects. Once a member of the all-conquering pub-team playing out of *The Albert* in West Didsbury in the Manchester League.

A gentle soul, but not across the chess board, where he has penchant for sneak attacks (like Roger Federer, he is modifying his game as he moves from the first bloom of youth).

Dave Dave

Not to be confused with Dave the Power, or some radio station for young fogies. When available, he is poached as top board for the second team, which always gives us far greater chances of success.

Dave Dave is famous for getting into and surviving the problems of nearly losing games for slow play. He is currently being outranked by his son, but is saved some embarrassment, because Kieran is unavailable for chunks of the season at present.

Why the name Dave Dave? It is his own chosen handle for differentiating himself from our club secretary, Dave the Power? Or is it something to do with needing an email address that hadn't been claimed by other members of the clan of Daves on the internet? Later in the season we were re-joined by yet another Dave, to add to the need for discriminating labels.

These players make up the core of the first team. But as they are often unavailable, Cap'n Phil has to draw on other players, from Paul's second team pool.

The names of these first team irregulars will also appear in subsequent accounts of the second team's battles. I am among them. I have a natural selection advantage due to my established habitat quite close to the borders of East Cheadle, which makes it easy for Phil to introduce me into home matches at a few minutes' notice.

Paul's Peashooter Army

Our second team captain Paul is one of the most positive people I have ever met. His enthusiasm inspires his team members to want to do their best. He is one of our secret weapons at East Cheadle. His oversized, titanium-white Paulmobile is a comforting sight, parked often in a space not large enough to accommodate it easily.

Paul always arrives in advance of the other team members giving himself plenty of time to scale the vary inaccessible flights of stairs to the playing rooms designed only for the very thin and able-bodied.

At times, and in contrast to Paul, I let negative thoughts into my mind, as I look at through the higher grades and current performances of our opponents before a match.

The league website almost always shows us to be heavily out-graded. To put not too fine a point on it, East Cheadle B team may be likened to an army advancing with our peashooters against a fortress bristling with well-drilled troops and Armourlight weapons.

Dave Dave plays as our top board as well as for the first team. All completely legal, particularly now the first team has acquired four players nominated because of their playing strength. He is the fifth strongest member of the club, and, like myself can play 'up' or remain among Paul's tightly-knit squad of committed fighters.

Also at Paul's disposal is the club secretary Dave the Power, rarely missing a match, rarely defeated, although inclined to draw many of his matches. This works well for a team that often needs every half point it can get.

Just as Dave Dave can play 'down' for us, Dave the Power can and does play 'up' for the first team. As Phil gently remained Paul during a period of absences, the First team has first pick. *Droit du Seigneur* stuff, if you ask me.

Then there is Cap'n Kev (Rtd.), Paul's predecessor as the leader of the B team, a player as tenacious as Dave the Power, with an encyclopaedic memory not just for his own pet openings, but those of many others in the league he has played against from time to time.

In the engine room, second row, or midfield (chose your metaphor) can be found myself, your unreliable narrator, capable of the occasional upset and the more frequent blunder.

I am there often in harness with Bill, long-distance cyclist, fell walker, sawbones extraordinaire, and newly appointed treasurer of the club's vast financial resources. Bill is often greeted by an opponent who has benefitted from his surgical skills. This gives a quite different meaning to the term *knowledge of a player's openings.*

Our captain Paul plays towards the bottom board and is able to keep an eye open for problems on or off the other five boards. This is relatively easy to do at East Cheadle where we arrange the boards in a row of six, with plenty of elbow room on the maroon baize-covered tables for clocks, score cards, drinks, spectacle cases and so on.

This is far from the case at less spacious venues, where the tables are often arranged in cramped and confusing fashion. This resulted in one of my worse mishaps later in the season, as we will see.

It is not unknown for a captain to assume the team to be winning and agree a draw only to discover too later he has been following a game from a different match being played in the room at the same time, or maybe squeezed between the match-boards and engaged in a friendly game arranged between two club members.

Because of our tendency to lose players through non-availability, Paul also has to call up others who have a part to play in our story. These are his territorial reserves drawn from the C team, ready to take up their muskets for the cause, as B team regulars fall in battle or become unavailable.

Myles' Musketeers

Some years ago, as numbers drifted downwards at East Cheadle, we found we were able to sustain two league teams, from a membership of around twenty players.

Then, after we merged amicably with Bramhall Beagles in 2014, membership rose to the mid-twenties, and we found we had a plethora of players mostly willing to play competitive chess. The influx offered players to strengthen the second team, but others were acquiring their taste for chess that suggested we should put forward a third team, to play in the third division of the league.

This has the advantage of being the only division from which relegation is not possible.

After discussions at the AGM it was agreed to try out a third team. The general feeling was that we should support more opportunities for players who might enjoy the cut and thrust of league competition.

It quickly became one of our secret assets. Players who had not played competitive chess before, found themselves enjoying the cut and thrust of league play.

The Dalai Lama and Dave the Power helped launch the venture. What was an experiment to some, turned out to produce an in-group loyalty found in great sporting teams from the Green Bay Packers under their legendary coach Vince Lombardy, to the *class of 1992* nurtured by Sir Alex Ferguson at Manchester United Football Club, and the Ryder Cup team of golfers which triumphed at Medina, inspired to *'do one for Seve'*.

Keith Archives, one of the new members acquired during the great Bramhall merger of 2013, quickly became an established team member. He acquired his discriminating name through the great historical work he produced on the Bramhall club, the original manuscript of which now can be found in the archives of the *Stockport Historical Society*. Keith, also brought many years of playing experience to the team.

The team also acquired Geoff Smyslov from Bramhall, (not to be confused with Geoff the Dalai Lama, or with Geoff Bristle).

It is heartening to realise that a successful international rugby team needs over six hundred 'caps' among its players. East Cheadle C has requisite levels of maturity, mustering nearly half that number of years of experience among them. This roughly matched those of the A and B sides.

An added ingredient for success was brought to the team by Captain Myles, another relatively new member to the club, who was fast-developing his chess playing and leadership skills.

He is assisted by Edwin who has also contributed posts which I draw from as the story develops. Young Keiran was another boost to team results, although he quickly became ineligible, as his grade soared to A and B team levels.

But with support from the club president (the Dalai Lama), the secretary (Dave the Power), and the occasional game from second team captain Paul, a surprising level of success has been achieved since its inception, and the team competes well with the more teams from the strongest clubs in the League.

Perhaps it has the added security net of knowing that there is no relegation to worry about from the third of the divisions in the league, which also applies to the Limit League competition.

The Limit League Legionnaires

Most sports clubs share an unwritten culture of admiration for their strongest players. The social reality seems pretty much the same in clubs catering for member's interests in rugby, tennis, golf, and I suspect many other pursuits. There is still some debate whether chess is a sport, a game, or a part-time pursuit for old codgers Be that is it may, the identity of chess clubs is not too different in the high status granted to the strongest players in more recognised sporting activities. This is a widely held view among social identity experts. If you prefer a simple empirical experiment, try getting a drink at the club bar before the club international who arrives after you.

Much of this is unconscious. I was largely unaware of the extent of my own elitist tendencies. These surfaced for me at the AGM as captain Keith of our new Limit League team modestly outlined their success. I wondered how many other members of the club were also unaware of the remarkable progress that had been made by the East Cheadle team since the inception of the league two years ago. Even now, it was treated as if its progress hardly compensated for the customary relegation battles of the teams in the loftier divisions.

In the past, discussion at each AGM was mostly about whether our membership could sustain more than two teams in our league. We competed with the other clubs for top players, wondering how we might attract them to East Cheadle. Two factors changed matters.

The first was the influx of members which occurred when we merged with Bramhall in 2013. We welcomed this as a possible justification for consolidating the need for maintaining a third team. I suspect most of the previous club members assumed that players not strong enough to make our third team didn't want to face the intense competition of league play.

The second was the dedication and considerable leadership skills shown by club officials. Treasurer Roger who for years had looked after our accounts while being unable to play more often than not because of his work shifts. Roy, an unofficial benefactor and social member now into his eighties, willing to open up the premises on a club night when team players were out of town. The telephone number as first point of contact on our outside notice board outside was Roy's, as was the noticeboard itself. And behind almost everything that happened, the figures of the President Geoff, and the Club Secretary David.

They are the driving forces for a culture which is all-embracing. If first and second team regulars were likely to miss club nights, the Dalai Lama would be there every Wednesday, playing in The Clubman competition he had designed to keep interest going throughout the season, for the members who were not league players. The complex scoring system gave points for playing whether you won or not. The idea was to reward *clubmanship* rather than awarding yet another prize to the those most able to win games.

David and Geoff made sure that everything possible would be done to ensure Bramhall members would be accepted as painlessly as possible. There was no 'tough bargaining' about whose premises were to be retained, or renaming the new club. East Cheadle had had enough of that in its great schism.

And the greatest and rather unheralded triumph was the emergence of the Limit League. The motion was pushed through the League's AGM with little concern, as it was seen to have little impact on the regulation of the three existing divisions. A mixture of Geoff's gentle persuasion, and David's somewhat more vigorous style, won the day.

The Fixtures Meeting

East Cheadle's team officials face the complicated task of avoiding fixture clashes which might deprive the various teams of their most wanted players.

They have to take into account when key members were away, and whether they could risk playing away matches in the hillier regions of the league in the middle of icy winter months.

For example, John, the regular board one of ECA team for several years, continues to have extended bird-watching breaks in a South African Safari park. Dave Dave, another much-prized player for both ECA and ECB teams has work commitments, often taking him out of the area.

Phil's own young family were taking second place too often for him to achieve a good chess/life balance he thought gloomily.

Paul has accepted his re-appointment as B Team captain after protesting he might not always justify his place. This is far from the case, as he always seems to score beyond his grading, and still deals calmly with the inevitable curious distractions that often crop up in match play.

The fixture-setting approach at the League AGM owes something to stock-market trading. Rival captains for each division milled around with electronic diaries at the ready, to trade off dates until all home and away fixtures had been agreed.

Phil's mood was not helped when he caught sight of Gladstone Whithers who had left East Cheadle after their last relegation. Gladstone had decamped to one of the strongest clubs in the league, and had reappeared now as their fixture secretary.

"Division One, again?" he said with an irritating smile which Phil read as more condescending than congratulatory.

"Division One. You didn't have to move club. You could have stayed, and helped us regain our premiership status" Phil said, paying more attention to his unfilled fixture slots still showing on his smart phone.

"It wasn't just for guaranteed division one play" Whithers replied, with just the slightest emphasis on guaranteed. "I wanted a club where I could have a drink afterwards"

"I though you always had to catch a train home" Paul commented.

"Not always. I sometimes stay over at my sister's place. Anyway, there's no place for quiet analysis at the Memorial Hall."

Phil and Paul had heard these arguments before. Should the club move from the premises they had stuck with for many years? There was a lot of affection for the familiar and functional premises. They were firmly in the heart of their local community, unlike some other clubs who had taken the pragmatic decision to move to the most pleasant and spacious playing location they could find at a reasonable rent.

But it was true that finding new members was a problem, particularly players strong enough for the first team. Even in comparison with other clubs, their recruitment record for women members was dire. The last one had left long before Paul became captain.

Recruitment of anyone under the age of thirty, was greeted with pleasure mixed with acceptance that the membership would still have more pensioners than youngsters below the age of fifty.

These two new recruits were a welcome relief, and strong enough to walk into the first team. But both Steve and Geoff enjoyed a drink after a game. Would they stay long at East Cheadle, particularly if the season was not successful enough to keep them playing in the premier league?

Whither's remarks had rattled the first team captain. In the Paulmobile returning to Cheadle, he mentioned his concerns to the second team Captain. Paul was quiet for a while. He normally viewed matters with the astonishing positivity needed to lead a team that consistent battled to stay in the second division of the league, rarely grappling their way to dizzy mid-table heights.

Maybe this year would be different. Maybe with the unexpected arrival of two new first team players, the trickle-down effect would make all the difference, Paul thought.

Stockport, who consistently took the league title, had moved to luxurious premises of The Conservative Club closer to Cheadle than to their own heartlands in the bustling metropolis of Stockport.

They had found a new home with plenty of parking. They could guarantee play for players of all levels in roomy premises. There was a warm and roomy bar area for post-match analysis. Even a woman member, Dr Baker, not just for show, but playing regularly at a league level, and who figures later in the story.

They don't need to seek out new members. Members peel off from other clubs to join them.

Paul drew from of his legendary well of positivity.

"A lot of our members like things as they are" he said. "We are not so much a chess club first, as a home from home."

This time it was Phil who remained silent. "One that's becoming more like a retirement home" he thought.

Although he and Paul were among the younger players at the club, barely into their forties, there were more members qualifying for a pensioner's subscription than those required to pay a full adult fee.

Welcome to the First Division

November 2015

From: Paul
To: Club members

As usual, this season the results of all our matches will appear on the club website. Team captains have agreed to supply reports which will appear on the website, as well as through our usual emails. I will also be covering these and chess matters on my blog.

It was a tough start to the league season for the first team. We had a home match against a strong Macclesfield team. We were heavily out-graded, and this was always going to be a tough slog.

Board 1

My opponent played a modest system and gave me no problems in the opening. When he started pushing pawns on the Queenside I thought I had better do something on the Kingside and started pushing pawns towards his King. Shortly afterwards I saw a little trick that seemed to win material. It almost did but he squirmed out of it and I ended up an exchange down for a pawn.

Materially that's about even and I was still doing quite well with my bishop pair but spent too long working out the complications. My position drifted and I lost on time in an inferior position. It was fun to cause my strong opponent some problems.

Board 2

John played sharply, but in the end, his enterprising play proved to be illusory he was left with a weak pawn in the centre and no attack. John's opponent created some play against John's king and finished strongly

Board 3

Our new young recruit Kieran, who as you may know is Dave Dave's offspring, was gradually being ground down. I didn't see the end of this game as I was too busy losing on time!

Board 4

One of our other newish recruits has been firing well. Geoff was put under pressure by his opponent's sharp King's Indian, but in the end managed to win. How? With a cheapo swindle (in Geoff's words!) but a point's a point. Our first this season, actually.

Board 5

Dave the Power (not to be confused with Dave Dave) was on board 5. David's *Fort Knox Defence* proved as good as its name, solid as a bank vault. It resisted all attacks until a slightly worse endgame, but sadly David was unable to hold on. Fort Knox was breached.

You will be learning more about this formidable defence and its leading advocate as the season progresses. Dave the Power takes over the captain's armband from me, if my other commitments mean I have to miss a match.

Board 6

Tudor played solidly in a *Queen's Pawn* game but ultimately had to settle for a draw.

All in all, a par result based on the respective ratings of the teams. The small matter of hosting Marple A in a fortnight may mean we will be getting most of our points after Christmas!

Postscript [T.R.]:

John's training sessions earlier in the year (*Openings you don't need to study)* has paid off for me. I have lost the appetite for study to keep up with theory.

I have a strong feeling that my opponents will be 'booked up' far better than I will be, in this division of the league. I will need to get out of the opening without losing quickly enough from a recent novelty to lower morale on the other boards.

Not quite what the pre-season optimism from our captains would have anticipated. Anyway, we are taking the hits against the strongest teams in the league early on, and maybe will have a chance to come on strong as the season progresses.

The President's Cup

The President's Cup is a new competition designed to give a chance to teams that are usually overwhelmed by the fire power of the strongest players in the league. This could work to our advantage at East Cheadle.

So it fell to Paul and his second division players to take on Stockport. He was to find himself caught up in a situation that had not been anticipated by the organizers at the league high command.

Paul's report on the club website explained what happened:

On Wednesday night we took on Stockport in the President's Cup. It looked a fairly even affair on paper, although they were particularly handy on the top two boards. We got off to a good start by winning the toss which meant we had three Whites to their two. Unlike the league, this match is over five not six boards

Keven was first to finish, and managed to earn a fairly quick draw against his higher graded opponent. He ended up with a better pawn structure and good knight against a ragged pawn structure and bishop pair. His stronger opponent offered a draw and Keven sensibly agreed in a very even position.

Dave Dave, looking relaxed after his recent successful chess tournament in the Channel Islands, finished soon after, with another excellent draw for us.

Then on board three was a battle of the academics. Dr Baker looked to have a winning position, but Tudor's bouncebackability came in to play again and in his own words he managed to swindle a very useful draw. [TR:

Did I really confess to that? At least the bragging rights between the Departments of Business and Pharm Studies are on hold for another season. Yes, we do brag, but very politely.]

On board four, Jim, another warrior returning from R&R in warmer climes, was playing against a very slow-looking *Queen Pawn* opening. It all looked a bit lifeless, and indeed after fifty moves it was pronounced dead, and a draw agreed.

Four games played - all draws. In this five-board contest it all depended on the two captains on the bottom board. Peter perhaps had a slight edge, but it was difficult for him to find a plan and in the meantime I was able to open up a file against his king and fill it with R and Q.

I had what looked like a winning attack. Unfortunately, (as confirmed by computer analysis by *Fritz*) there was no breakthrough, and all the excitement petered out into an opposite-colour bishop draw.

Much checking of the rules. Their captain Peter and I decided we didn't know which side had won. In fact, it turns out there is nothing in the rules for the new competition about a Cup result of all draws.

So, the match ended in a stalemate. We have agreed to have a replay at their place as soon as we can fix a date.

Reality check for the Second Team

Paul creeps home around midnight after the first league match of the season for the second team.

He files his report for the club website before retiring to bed. The pre-season elation had received its first reality check. Here is his summary of the exciting and unexpected happenings which kept him out so late:

It was a late finish on Wednesday night at East Cheadle. I rolled home getting on for midnight with the wife saying “where've you been ‘til this time?”

I replied “erm ... well...it was the digital clocks. One of them was set to number 3 instead of number 18.” Like some members of the team, I don’t think she understood what had happened. More of that in a bit.

Our first opponents were from the ancient silk town of Macclesfield. Their A and B teams are going to be strong again this season. They were missing two or three players, but still put out a very decent team.

I was first to finish. My opponent had played a flawed opening, but instead of winning a piece I blundered badly. One down and five to play.

Nick on board six then got a draw in a game he was never going to lose. He could not make headway against a defensive setup designed for opponents to ‘bite on granite’. Nick did not oblige.

Tudor played well in his game and was looking good but just slipped up at the end.

[TR: Very kind, Paul. I made a complete Horlicks of a position and wasted two hours of decent effort previously with a lapse of concentration I have warned against, in my *Chess for beginners* talk. My lapses are coming more frequently than they used to, and Paul has sympathetically allowed my gentle slide down the board-order to continue.]

Our only full point of the night was won by Bill. He staved off a strong attack and then managed to gang up on a pawn and won it. The only problem was that his opponent had an hour left on his clock and Bill only two minutes.

That quickly reduced to two seconds (!) before Bill, with nerves of steel, made his move. His opponent tried to rush things and replied immediately, hoping to force a win on time, but forgot he had left his queen *en prise*. Bill took it, and with the wonders of the Fischer timing had a simple win. Well done Bill.

Meanwhile, Keven was playing his favourite opening, and as usual got a very good game out of it. Unfortunately, he overcooked it a bit which lost material but he managed to get his queen very active and looked likely to force a draw with perpetual, before his opponent found a way of wriggling out of it, and went on to win.

So that meant we had lost the match, but the drama was by no means over.

Dave Dave's long awaited debut for the B team was memorable to say the least. Our ringer from the A team set up a very double-edged game with opposite side castling. The Macclesfield board one had strong pressure with the heavy pieces.

Dave Dave had this well-covered, and had more space on the queenside and with a better pawn structure he looked maybe in a slightly better position. Near the end he still had twenty minutes on his clock, with his opponent only having two (maybe Dave Dave will not be so pressed for time at division two level of play).

It still became a real scramble and mysteriously his opponent's flag went (Dave had only eight seconds left!).

That shouldn't have happened in the Fischer Chess time control which adds on a ten second increment per move, should it?

It transpired that the clock had been set up on standard time with an extra 10 seconds in total (setting 3) rather than 10 seconds per move (setting 18). Oops.

As with Bill, the electronic clocks are playing a big part in the fun.

The atmosphere turned rather tense. Dave Dave quite rightly claimed a win on time. With hindsight his opponent should have stopped his clock before the flag fell, to point out something was wrong, but of course in the heat of battle this is not easy.

Compromise was reached, if not harmony restored. It was eventually agreed to play a blitz finish from the last agreed sensible board position with ten minutes each player and a ten second increment (this time, with the correct clock setting).

This was very tough on Dave. It's no picnic on board one in this division at the best of times, but great credit to Dave for agreeing to carry on playing, in a game he thought he had already won.

To make matters worse his opponent now found a much better continuation, although Dave managed to equalize skilfully under extreme pressure.

A pity Dave didn't go on to win, but at least he didn't lose.

[TR: Another example of Paul's positivity.

So after all that chaos over time controls, we have lost our first league match of the new season, with the final score of 2 – 4.

I think there are going to be interesting very matches ahead of us.]

Our Hidden Strengths

In cannot be denied that most teams we meet in our League have younger, fitter, stronger players than we do, and often play in more spacious premises.

Perhaps other teams also have players who are more single-minded in search of every possible point than we are.

Such an analysis would miss one important and hidden ingredient. It is something in the very culture of the club. You can breathe it in the air, as one management guru described it to me. The essence of a warm, welcoming, even life-enhancing culture. This is epitomised by members who have worked tirelessly for the club in good times and bad. It is particularly exemplified by Dave the Power, (not to be confused with Dave Dave and the club President, The Dalai Lama) who unlike our other Daves is hardly old enough to claim his pensioner's bus pass.

Both have acquired wisdom and respect through the years. It would be simplistic to try pinning down their impact with a simple label. [Note to any students reading. You might want to check out recent literature on leaders guided by a moral compass. Also, the Herman Hesse mysticism which mutated into the Servant Leadership movement.]

David (Dave the Power) is an angular man. Thin, with the aquiline feature which despite absence of the distinctive moustache reminds me of grainy photographs of General Montgomery addressing his troops from the top of a tank. Yes, Dave the Power could do that, waving his league documents and nicely bound book he records his games in.

The Dalai Lama is also enormously organized, as befits a former manager of one of our imperial age industries. In contrast to David he is a burly avuncular figure. He persists in arranging the world to deal with his refusal to learn to type (not just on a PC, but on one of those mechanical thingies). He makes up for this by sending beautifully hand-written communications to the members as needed. He has been a monumental figure in the club holding various official positions.

A few years ago he was playing in a match which promised a rare victory for the B team. Under the pressure, perhaps, his opponent was taken unwell and had to stop playing. Given the opportunity, David would probably have found a rule covering the unfortunate incident. Geoff took his own decision. "I wasn't really winning" he said "so I offered him a draw".

Both David and Geoff went through hip operations recently and recovered without fuss, although Geoff has had to postpone his beloved cycling trips into the Peak District's scenic byways.

Our own influx of stronger players comprises a group of members who would have been made welcome in every club in the league. We welcomed them, in my considered judgement, warmly but no more warmly as we welcome all other prospective members.

John told me at the regular season-ending social evening and quick-play event how he had found its atmosphere more than compensates for our less than sparkling league performances.

Dave the Power and Dalai Lama as was Major Max before them, are examples of a declining species of amateur gentlemen competing against the advance of more single-minded competitors.

As a matter of fact, there is a section about the spirit of the game in our league rules. Geoff in particular would have ignored that if it seemed to point him in the wrong direction according to his moral compass. Dave would probably have a copy of the rules and seen that East Cheadle was not going to be unfairly denied a half point by a player unable to continue.

I was at a tournament once where a player collapsed in play. It was later proved that the collapse had been a fatal one. He tournament director acted rapidly according to the rules. He moved swiftly though the boards and players most of whom were unaware of what had happened.

“Stop his clock” he was heard to say. I imagine Geoff would have wanted to check the player’s health, and then to award him a posthumous draw.

Why I am not a Grandmaster

I play chess from time to time with Dave Sampras who is a coach at the Northern Tennis Club Didsbury (aka *The Wimbledon of the North*). He appears in my monograph *Tennis Matters*, as the latest in a line of gurus trying to help me achieve my life-quest of acquiring a decent forehand.

He recently asked me how many of our members at East Cheadle were chess masters, and whether I was one of them. I said that we had several players who have beaten masters in competitive play.

It was modesty which prevented me from mentioning my triumph against the New Zealand master Bob Wade, during a simultaneous display he was giving at the British Championships in Leicester in the late 1950s.

I found myself explaining to Coach David how fate has contributed to my own shortcomings in that respect. (He has sporting bragging rights. I competed in the *U18 British Chess Championships*, he won the *U18s Tennis Championships* at Wimbledon)

This is what I told him, demonstrating with a chess board borrowed from behind the bar of the tennis club.

I have given up chess four times since I left school, I said. Each coincided with a change of geographic location. Maybe I was never completely serious about quitting, because most of my increasing collection of chess books would always come with me.

Today, what remains of my mini-library reveals a secret of an archaeological kind. A great schism occurred in chess towards the end of the last century. Before the disruption lies the age of *descriptive notation* in the English-speaking chess world. It is still found in movies about chess. in which typically a player, perhaps the villain, will say in suitably sinister tones. "*Pawn to the king's fourth*". This is accompanied by a dramatic move forward of a central pawn.

to which the hero might reply "*Pawn to the king's fourth*".

A non-chess player might exclaim *"Oi! He's just done that move!"*

Indeed. Well spotted. Strictly speaking each player should have said "*I move my pawn on my king's file to my fourth rank on said file.*"

In this set of two opening moves, each pawn is moved up the board two squares, producing an *empasse*, each blocking further progress of the other.

If the game is being recorded, (which it never is in these movies, not even in Bergman's famous chess game between the knight and the shrouded figure of death), the moves would have been written as

1 P-K4 1 P-K4 on the first line of the score sheet. The moves are descriptions from the point of view of each of the players, hence the name of the notation.

It is easily traced to its ancestor, the *early descriptive* form found in the great *Handbook of Chess*, written in the 1880s by the English champion *Howard Staunton*. In that form, it was rather more laborious to write down. I showed David my own prized copy of the handbook, and carefully opened it at random. I found a typical game being described. In those days, compression was ignored, and the first moves I came across were

10 K.B. to Q.Kt's 5th 10 P to Q.R.'s 3rd

I explained how I had been taught to write them in the modern compressed form as

10 B-Kt5 10 P-QR3.

But the early and modern descriptive approaches already had a rival in other parts of the world known as *the algebraic notation*. This avoided the apparent Anglo-Saxon silliness of having pieces apparently being moved to the same square.

In algebraic notation, all the squares were numbered in a grid starting at a1, the (bottom left as white would see it, top right as black could see it).

Staunton's example would have been written as

10 Bb5 10 a6

In the 1980s, the international chess body FIDE announced that all official games were to be recorded using the algebraic notation. It must be said that FIDE has from time to time shown tendencies found in their football equivalent FIFA, but that's another story. This monstrous denial of human rights left a generation of British chess players struggling to sort out their a5s from their QR4s.

Reluctantly, all chess publishers that had preferred the descriptive notation began to convert to algebraic notation.

The consequences are there to be seen on my book shelves. Only a few dear favourites remain in descriptive formats. Older publications have been rewritten in the algebraic system.

The latest descriptive notation book I can find in my collection is the classic *My Memorable Games* by Bobby Fischer, published in 1972.

From then on, it has been algebraic all the way. And it turned out to be far more convenient for pesky computers to manipulate chess data, which is another story.

FIFA's edict contributed to the great demise of the descriptive notation, the chess equivalent of the disappearance of the dinosaurs.

Meanwhile, I know that I am not alone in struggling because I was brought up speaking and writing in descriptive. My own scoresheet still often shows numerous corrections, often still ending up looking as if I have played a different game from my opponent.

I then told David that I liked to think it is one reason why I never became a grandmaster. That is not quite true. The main reason is a lack of talent. But I didn't want to confess to that.

The Charnley Cup

The Charnley Cup is the most prestigious knock-out competition in the league. East Cheadle have sometimes played above their ratings in typical giant-killer style. With their strengthened team, hope runs high.

Former captain and distinguished club secretary Dave the Power took charge in the absence of Phil, and filed the following match report:

From: David
To: Club members

East Cheshire A team kicked off the season with a Charnley Cup home match against Chorlton. Despite two of our top three players being unavailable, and Chorlton fielding a strong team, we gave a good account of ourselves.

Dave Dave was the first to finish with a draw. Then Tudor with another draw. I didn't have much time to watch their games.

Then I also accepted an offered draw, perhaps too hastily, but I had less time left than my opponent and the fairly blocked position looked as if it could go either way for whoever opened it up.

This gave me time to watch the others. All the top three had good chances. However, Steve, faced with an attack on his king, took shelter behind two pawns with a rook to help, but his opponent invaded his position and advanced a deadly rook's pawn to finish Steve off.

Kieran took a draw in a late middle game position with not much prospect of winning against a very strong opponent.

That left Geoff with the unenviable task of saving face. Sadly, even a win would still mean we lost due to the board elimination rule.

His opponent seemed to view the whole thing as a bit of a joke, until Geoff's fine endgame play took it down to a tight ending.

With both players needing the ten second increments to stay in the game, both players were having to move almost instinctively, and was very exciting to watch.

Geoff avoided all the tricks and traps his now fully-focussed opponent tried, and finally when he captured the pawn his opponent gave up.

We lost, but a good start by Geoff and Kieran in the top team.

Enter Houdini

It is often difficult to establish the authenticity of a historic event. This one is different, as I played a central part in it, together with our distinguished Club secretary. It tells the story of how Houdini entered into the folk-lore of East Cheadle Chess Club.

It came about during one of those periods when both of our teams were playing in the second division. This has advantages. We are bound to win some points in the four fixtures in which the two club teams meet. Also, all four matches are in effect played at The Memorial Hall. In each, one is the nominated home team, playing white on the even numbered boards. The other is the away team, playing white on odd numbered boards.

The disadvantage is that it can get a little boring. There is some scope for mixing up the players, as with the exception of the very strongest and weakest are of roughly equivalent strengths. For some reason the captains agreed to do just that. As a consequence, it is the only match I have ever played match for which I am not sure which team I was on.

I do know that my opponent was the formidable Dave the Power, renowned for his reluctance to lose. Hence his infamous preference for draw-at-all-cost openings, and it must be said, a high proportion of draws at the end of a season.

The captains' plan worked out well. There was little difference in the two hybrid AB teams. Nor were there games in which bizarre events contributed to a freak result. as seems to happen rather often at East Cheadle.

As the evening drew on, my team (whichever one it was) began to shed points. David continued to grind away. Then, for not the first time in recent seasons, I had a lapse of concentration. David gleefully snaffled a pawn and started playing more confidently.

Most of the games had finished. Other players were boxing and removing the sets and clocks, and dismantling tables as quietly as they could. A few came to watch silently, but concluded it would take quite a while for David to complete the win. Only a win for me could now rescue a draw for my team.

Eventually, everyone except the two players had left. Should I accept the inevitable and resign? After all, I didn't even know which team I was playing for. Then I remembered Houdini.

It was David who had mentioned that great escapologist at the start of the previous season. I had begun with one of the most amazing sequences of wins from losing positions ever to have happened to me. David had watched, as week after week I had recovered from stupid mistakes. I guess David, who rarely makes such mistakes, must have felt that fate was smiling disproportionately on me.

Eventually after one cheapo, I got up from the board to hear David exclaiming “He's escaped again. He's like Houdini.”

Would David be even more cautious now, in light of his beliefs about the unfair dollups of good fortune that had been coming my way? Maybe, but there was no other way to play. Eventually I found something in the position that gave me a chance. A move that seemed to lead me into a trap laid by David. So I had to appear to be forced into the trap that David had laid for me.

If David noticed, he only had to do nothing compromising, and I was toast. My plan was technically unsound because with correct play I was going to lose quickly. But the prize for him overlooking what I was up to was not just for me to draw, but to win from a lost position.

A few moves where nothing much happened, and when I was appearing to running out of reasonable moves. Soon there would be only one move for me to play. David could force the move that appeared to lose for me, but actually may lose for him.

I tried not to look too hard, or look away too innocently.

He fell for the trap. I spent a few moments looking to see if I had missed anything. If I had, I would resign immediately.

I hadn't, and played the winning move. David stared at the position, looked up to the ceiling and then down again at the board.

"Houdini" he barked.

I must have looked rather shiftily at him. We put the sets and table away without saying much, and left the deserted hall, turning the lights out as we went. David was still shaking his head at the spirit of Houdini which had appeared and ruined his evening.

Marple comes to Town

November 2015

Captain Phil's report for the club's website

After a tough first match against Macclesfield A, there was no respite for ECA this week, with a home game against the heavyweights of Division 1, Marple A.

Marple had several of their top players missing, but with a very strong top two boards graded a master's level 220-210 they were always favourites.

Here is how it went.

Steve on top board played a solid defence as black and steadily swapped off pieces, entering a Bishop ending where he had a slightly worse pawn structure but good chances of holding. However, he allowed his Bishop to get trapped and had to give it up for two pawns. This was similar to the memorable time when the great Bobby Fischer played such a move at the start of his world championship match with Boris Spassky.

Although it looked like his extra pawns may give him some chances, Steve's king was tied to the defence of some weak kingside pawns. Just like Bobby, all those years ago, he eventually lost.

John on board two played his normal *Queen's Gambit* and got a level position but didn't manage to create much pressure. His opponent started to make threats on the kingside but John successfully neutralised his opponent's initiative. In the endgame, John's king went on the rampage. It looked like an upset could be on the cards but with strong defence from black a draw was agreed.

My opponent played a quiet system against my favourite *King's Indian Defence* and surprised me with some early pawn pushes on the Queenside. I got my pieces in a bit of a tangle but managed to defend against persistent Knight threats but I was able to simplify to a draw.

Board four. Keiran shares a family penchant for backward e pawns. His opponent exploited it in textbook fashion as in the classical book "*My System*" by Nimzowich.

On the next board, Dave Dave played his favourite *Dutch Defence* and achieved a very comfortable position but his opponent played actively enough and with Dave short on time (as happens) a draw was agreed.

Finally, Dave the Power had a solid opening which didn't seem to yield any real threats. He ended up a pawn down with several weak pawns to defend. Ultimately David could not hold the endgame.

So a tough match, and a fair result in our 1.5 – 4.5 defeat. There is no respite, as we complete our tour of the top teams in two weeks, with a home match against Holmes Chapel.

We should not be too worried, as we are taking our pain early in the season against the toughest opponents.

Don't Do as I Do ...

From: T.R.
To: Club members

Our Secretary David has asked me would I give a talk at the club, following the brilliant and successful ones from John last year.

Unlike John, my credentials are that I have lost in a large number of ways, and have collected a list of rules that may help you avoid doing the same.

The top guns of the first and second teams are playing away, which is a pity as some of them could have commented on their own experiences.

Here are my rules, which I will illustrate at the start of next week's club night, drawing on a few of my crop of recent blunders.

When I break them, most often, bad things happen. So this is a starter-kit of *don't do as I do, do as I would be more advised to do*. The principles are to be found in any introductory book on chess.

Rule 1. *Do not fall behind in development.*

This means do not move the same piece frequently, when other pieces remain in their original positions.

Rule 2. *Don't move pawns without thinking about how the opponent will attack them*

Pawns can't move backwards. When you move a pawn try to visualize your 'chain' of pawns, how the structure may persist, and how it may be broken. The great Nimzowich teaches us how to attack pawn chains at the weakest point.

Rule 3. *Beware of simplifying moves*

Unless you are winning, you should avoid simplifying exchanges. More often than not, they favour the second player. (Check this out on your games with a Search Engine. See how the advantage swings.)

Rule 4. *Calculate most when you think the position has become complicated, but not for too long*

Some positions do not need a lot of calculations. For example, if your opponent has been playing the move you expected. These are balanced positions, with pawns defended, pieces coordinated. Decide on how to strengthen the position. Coordinate pieces to avoid under-protection, and over-burdened pieces. These are where tactics come in.

Rule 5. *Practice plan B*

A plan B might be a change of strategy. If you have made a mistake you may need to find a plan that you hadn't thought of. For example, sometimes if you lose a pawn it leaves your opponent's position slightly weakened. Look how to exploit it as if you made a pawn sacrifice.

Remember, most games have chances for the player with an inferior position. A losing game is different from a lost game. Your opponent may relax waiting for the game to be over in their favour

Rule 6. *Avoid time trouble*

Try to play safe and simple 'holding' moves when you are in a familiar position, to keep up with your opponent's time. If you do get into time trouble, try to guess your opponent's move and use your opponent's time. If you have guessed his move, then reply quickly.

Rule 7 *Move quickly, but not too quickly*

You can sometimes get carried away. Don't rush into winning material if you can eliminate threats first. Put your king where you want it to be, avoiding nasty checks.

Other things worth thinking about

Practice looking for *candidate moves*. Your chosen candidate move should 'feel' right. Almost always you will not be able to calculate to be completely certain that you have chosen the move.

Hope that has not deterred anyone from turning up for practice next week.

Presidents Cup: The Replay

This was the night of one of my worse chess losses. Captain Paul reported the replay of the President's Cup match against Stockport, who were, as expected, ready for us this time. I added my own painful comments to Paul's summary of a very bad night.

From: Paul
To: Club members

Unfortunately, there wasn't much Christmas cheer for us last night, as we went crashing out of the President's Cup in the replayed 1st Round tie. I turned up last minute, lost the coin toss, then wrongly advised our team what colour they were playing - not a good start.

Tudor, promoted to board one, was first to finish. His comments are:

"League record loss in four moves, which is nearly as rapid as if I had engineered a fools' mate! Sat down expecting to play white. Switched seats to take the black pieces after some confusion, and did not 'reset' for black. But I was happy to play a variation of the Alekhine (come and get me if you can) defence which I know very well.

Was thinking of and played its fifth move when I hadn't played the fourth. Grateful opponent takes a knight I had left en prise. One minute on my clock. Resigns."

It was a shame for Tudor, particularly as he's been in terrific form recently [TR: Thanks, Paul.]

Bill finished next and his trusted *Caro-Kann Defence* got him a fine draw with a solid performance. Keven got what looked like a good positon against a *Queens Indian*, but his opponent found a resource later on to win.

Nick looked in control in his match but it wasn't quite as simple as it looked and he lost his way when trying to press for a quicker win. I had a decent position, but was happy to accept a draw when it was offered.

So, after the record-breaking rule-challenging excitement of the first tie, we went under and out to tough opposition, 1-4

Thanks to everyone for support. We still have half a season to make up for our bad start.

See you all in January.

More Reality Testing

The five-move loss has kicked me for six. At one level I can laugh it off. It is *sooo* stupid, that it can be seen as a once-in-a-lifetime anomaly.

Unless …

Unless it's more than an anomaly. Maybe it's part of a deeper darker decline in my chess. Worse, part of a decline in my general faculties.

My darkest fears surfaced when a friend confided in me that he had been regularly visiting a mutual acquaintance who had been a strong league player in the 1960s. "A few years ago he could still beat me" my friend said. "Now, I have to set out the pieces at the start. He sets up the board with the rooks upside down. And he forgets whose move it is."

I forget moves, not from that dreadful disease, although I increasingly forget what the score is at tennis, or what I went into the bathroom to do.

"It's not my general play" I confided in Paul. "I think I'm playing as well as I was thirty years ago. It's more I can't concentrate. Particularly after about a couple of hours at the board. And I don't analyse as much. I rely on experience, knowing the feel of a position. That's OK most of the time at the level of competition I play against. It even means I rarely take long over my moves."

Paul continued his genuine positive take on things. "But you fight back. That takes concentration"

"It's just too unreliable. It's only an extreme example of how playing level declines. Even grandmasters, with one or two exceptions, drop off and quit in their forties. I'm long past that."

I was thinking of that winning streak. "Even my wins come because I blunder in about one game in three. Some years ago I kept records. I might make a one-move blunder two or three times a season. Now it's closer to on in two or three games. Even the Houdini job on Dave the Power was necessary because of a blunder I made."

"Everyone goes through spells, bad trots."

I was unmoved. "Kind of you to say. But this seems more like a one-way street to me. You should think about playing me as low down in the board order as is possible."

But I knew board order would not make a difference. I was someone who could not be relied on to deliver a win in a tight situation any more however strong or weak the opposition was. And it was becoming clear that the East Cheadle teams would be in tight situations at the end of the playing season, however optimistic Paul and Phil had been at the start.

Chess Blindness

Something wrong with my eyes, which is why I can't see the chessboard clearly. So, what do I do? Go to the Optician, obviously.

But not straight away. Instead, I talk it over during a lesson with a tennis coach. I didn't mention chess, just saying I had been thinking what might be stopping me hit a proper forehand.

It took about two minutes to confirm my suspicions. Coach David (i.e. the tennis David) told me to put down my racquet and stand a few feet from the net. Then he took me through a training activity I had seen him use with the under-eight classes.

"I want you to catch the ball in both hands."

He tossed the ball gently to my left side. I fumbled it, but eventually grasped it safely.

"Now to the right."

Time stood still then went backwards as I moved towards the ball. For a moment I was at school, playing pretend rugby with a tennis ball before classes started.

I moved to my right and caught the ball smoothly, ready to swerve and run towards the goal line with it. I was elated. I was at Cardiff Arms Park, playing for Wales.

"Good. Now, to your left again."

The difference was obvious. This time, I clutched at the ball and it fell out on my grasp.

After a few more attempts it was obvious why I had struggled with tennis shots to my left.

"We can work on that."

Coach David is as positive as Paul at East Cheadle. We moved on, with me attempting to catch the balls in one hand as they were gently tossed to me, first to my left, then my right. The results were pretty much the same as before. Reasonable to the right, clumsy to the left.

David then took me further back, beyond the service T, and used his racquet to feed me longer balls, concentrating on my left side. I had to imagine the catch was taking place with arms extended for a racquet shot. As a left-hander, the balls would be going to my infamous and wayward forehand.

It again took only a few balls for me to realize I have been playing for years with a zone in which I was not, could not, follow the ball. This was roughly before it bounced.

"We can work on it" he repeated. He was still in Paul-positivity mode.

"What can I do next?" I asked.

His answer sounded less positive. "See an Optician as soon as possible" he replied.

Fate was Unkind

Sunday, 13 December 2015

Phil looked at the email he had received from his stand-in captain Dave the Power. He decided against embellishing the blunt assessment of the result, and topped and tailed Dave the report before posting it to the website:

ECA continued their tricky start to the season with a home fixture against Holmes Chapel last week. I unfortunately could not make it, so here is David's report:

We were soundly beaten by Holmes Chapel who fielded a strong team. Fate was also a bit unkind, because by 7:45 pm we only had three players. Dave Dave and Kieran were faced with a substantial time deficit when they eventually got through the traffic gridlock, even though their opponents voluntarily delayed starting their clocks until 7.45.

At one stage, Dave Dave had less than 10 seconds on his clock, yet he still played another twenty moves or more, and got a draw. Apparently both father and son had expected their opponents to play the King's Indian, and had prepared accordingly, only to find different openings when they eventually started.

I lost first. For once my Fort Knox King's position was mercilessly destroyed, my opponent having seen one move further ahead than me. Tudor won so easily he could afford to ignore the offer of a Rook at one stage, unable to believe that it was safe to take it (or not seeing the offer at all?).

Kieran and Geoff were being steadily ground down and in spite of surviving until nearly 10.45 pm were faced with overwhelming pawn majorities. Steve considered himself lucky to obtain the draw on top board, but to the onlookers he seemed to have it all under control.

So another tight match but another defeat, East Cheadle 2 : Holmes Chapel 4. Time to recharge batteries over the break, and prepare for the New Year.

T.R: Postscript

David's report via Phil has me worried. Am I playing so much on automatic pilot that I miss the offer of a Rook? I can remember roughly when the oversight might have occurred. I was in the fortunate position of having my opponent completely helpless. I was ahead in material and had a slow but inevitable plan underway to close out the game. If I had seen the play to collect a free Rook I might have ignored it, as I was trying to avoid thinking. But if I missed the generous offer it was another example of me losing concentration at a crucial stage in a game.

Phil (or is it David) is right. Leave it until the New Year.

Dave Dave Springs into Action

Stung by poor results, (and perhaps by the inevitable progress of chess-playing son over chess-playing dad who taught him the moves), Dave Dave sets out on a course of self-improvement that may yet rescue East Cheadle's season.

From: Dave Dave
To: Club members

Regarding chess improvement. As some of you may know my own chess reached an all-time low last season when my grade dropped to 141.

Clearly I had to make some changes if this downward slump was to be halted.

The result has been 31 long-play games since August with only three losses and a projected January grade of 164 provided that all the league games are put in for grading. Still trying to decide if I should continue with my improvement plan, or retire from chess now, whilst the going is good.

Merry Christmas
Dave Dave

Another Way of Losing

From: T.R.
To: Club members

As Dave Dave continues his dedicated efforts to make 2016 a rewarding chess year for himself and us, I dig into my extensive file of *how not to do it incidents* which have not been mentioned on the Phil's blog. Maybe my story will be of help to other club members as the season develops.

Incidentally, in his steep plummet to a grade of 141, he is still only approaching the grades some of us still are reaching in our bathyspheric journeys of decline.

Here is my account of a recent incident which illustrates my deep diving.

In a visit to a nearby club for a league encounter, I found myself in what might be called a cramped position. Not cramped on the board, but squashed physically with the small table dangerously close to my abdomen.

These circumstances arose because there were two teams were playing in a room hardly large enough to accommodate one.

Against a strong player, I was doing alright on the clock and the board. My bishops were nicely poised controlling much space, albeit positioned rather close to my belly button.

Then disaster struck.

I played an obvious move with one of the bishops which I expected would lead to a drawish late middle-game. As I touched the preferred cleric, I knocked it over and moved the other bishop to the intended square.

My opponent pointed out with unseemly enthusiasm that I had made an illegal move. He claimed his right that I make a legal move with the bishop I had just propelled not quite diagonally up the board. Hope you are following this.

I explained that I would never have made such a dumb move and showed him my intended one. He continued to claim his rights. The best I could do was enter a losing endgame. After some red-mist stuff from me I played on, and lost in a rather frosty atmosphere, contributing to the catalogue of ways in which it is possible to lose a chess game.

Moral of tale. Get comfortable, make sure there is a decent gap on the touch-line closest to the abdomen side of the board. If you bash a piece over, repeat *J'adoube* several times before completing a move.

Always carry a charged hip-flask for medicinal purposes.

In my Dreams

I am working through my pain at the unfortunate loss of a point, and in such an undignified fashion. I fell into a dream about how the evening might have ended. It gives me some consolation to replay the event with some control over the outcome.

I had been researching the great forensic scientist Edmond Locard, known as the French Sherlock Holmes. George Simenon attended Locard's lectures and drew on them to give authenticity to his Inspector Maigret cases.

Locard propounded a maxim known as *Locard's exchange principle*, which states that every contact leaves a trace. A gun fired leaves residues that are revealed in the hair, on skin, and most markedly on the thumb and forefinger of the shooter. Unfortunately for the criminal investigator, and fortunately for the law breakers, the residues can be transferred. Not just to another person using the gun, but by the act of shaking hands, or other physical contact.

Locart's principle set me off considering another version of the unfortunate incident. I have the white pieces and start a queen's pawn game which my opponent turns into a *Benoni* defense. This leads to a complex manoeuvring game after Black sacrifices a pawn.

Note for chess historians: For many years I thought the Benoni defence was named after a tournament held in the South African town of the same name. In checking, I find the name has been attributed to a seventeenth century German expert who studied chess to help him deal with his moods of depression.

In describing a gambit for black, he called it the Benoni, a rather wry comment, aware of the biblical reference to ben Oni, the son of sorrow.

The physical conditions we are playing underplaying area are rather cramping, with little elbow or knee room. I slide my recording sheet half-way under the board to my right to secure it. Much of the play is to my left (the queen's side of the board where the pawn had been offered up and snaffled by me).

My two bishops have established as a formidable attacking battery. My opponent threatens one of them. As I move to deal with the threat, the precarious balancing act of the chess clock, chess board, my score sheet, and cramped knees beneath collapse. I touch the pieces, knocking over both bishops and a pawn (collateral damage).

I replace the pieces. But I have already made a big mistake. My eagle-eyed opponent notices I have touched not the bishop I had intended, but its fellow cleric in the melee. I have also failed to utter the absolution '*j'adoube*', chess language for *sorry, just putting the pieces right.*

My opponent is convinced that I had blundered and then contrived the disruption to get away with playing a different move. He thinks I'm cheating. The *touch a piece move a piece* rule is invoked. A discussion is initiated with the two team captains. It is left up to my opponent to claim his justice according to the law, with me muttering about pounds of flesh, justice and mercy.

He claims his rights. I have no decent move with the 'wrong' bishop so I resign, expressing disappointment at his ignoring what is touched on briefly as I in the league handbook.

That. As I recall, is what happened. But now, with thoughts of Locard in my mind, I replay the incident.

In the middle of the dispute, the door to the playing room bursts open. Members of the CIA, (the elite Chess Investigation Agency), rush in.

"CIA. Nobody move. Just slowly stop the clocks." *Scene of Chesscrime Assistants* (SOCAs) isolate the overburdened table, with me and my glaring opponent inside the tapes they have strung around it.

"We need swabs from all of you. Starting with you two guys, and then the chess pieces."

We and chess pieces are swabbed. Then the same treatment for the other players, uncomplaining and fearful of the reputation of the Serious Chess Offenses department of FIDE.

Several months later, the case goes to the FIDE court. The forensic evidence is clear. It shows without doubt I had touched both bishops, but the wrong bishop first.

A defence plea that it was an accident was accepted, and I was charged with the lesser crime of being guilty of interruption to a chess game, and sentenced to a season's community work writing up the reports of our league matches.

It will be a long season.

I Investigate the Blunder

Another far more disturbing possibility explaining the two bishop bungling has struck me. At present, it no more than speculation, but I think there may be something going seriously wrong with my eyesight.

I reluctantly reached that conclusion after a particularly frustrating game of tennis. I was playing as badly as ever. In the warm-up session. I could hardly hit the ball over the net. Things improved marginally when the game started, and I could compensate by playing every shot as a backhand.

After chess, tennis has been the most important sporting activity in my life. I suppose there has rarely been a week since my schooldays when I have not spent some time playing or watching tennis.

When I started self-publishing, the first sports book I wrote was *Tennis Matters*, about my love of the game. Its running joke was my life-long failure to hit a decent forehand, regardless of the efforts of six different coaches.

What I hadn't considered in the book, or since, until today, was the possibility that my right eye has increasingly become dominant, while my left is leaving all the hard work to its ocular partner. In tennis this is known as lazy partner syndrome.

As I am a natural left-hander, my tennis forehand is probably over-reliant on my right eye. It may be, that I have been operating with monocular vision at present.

And not just on the tennis court. When I clumsily knocked over the chess pieces, I did so with my left hand. The pieces were on the left, as I was looking at the board.

This gives me pause to reflect.

It is no longer a joking matter. My suspicion is that I have a cataract developing which is increasingly affecting my vision, my tennis, and even my chess. It took a bad game of tennis and a clumsy chess move to draw attention to something more serious.

The obvious sensible thing is to consult with an expert. I will dig out that reminder from my optician saying that I am due for a check-up, which I ignored when it arrived a few months ago.

A New Year Dawns

January 2016

A new year dawns. I have made an appointment with my local optician.

The A team faces another of the league heavyweights.

Phil's report of another loss gives me more apprehension about the likely outcome of the remaining matches in the second half of the season:

From: Phil
To: all members

ECA 1.5 Stockport A 4.5

Another tough match for ECA, and once again the rating difference showed, and we were soundly beaten. Life in the top division sure is challenging.

I had black on board one. I played my favoured *King's Indian Defence*. I carried out the usual central break with e5 but this only opened the diagonal for White's Bishop on f4. My central pawn advances proved to be weak and White's Queenside pressure eventually won a pawn. In the end, I lost more pawns as I ran out of time. A typical grind against a strong player.

Steve played a b3 (queenside fianchetto) system against the *French Defence* but got into trouble early on with his weak dark squares produced on the Queenside. Eventually Steve's king got stuck in the centre, and a textbook pawn thrust enabled Black to gobble up some pawns to win.

Kieran played a solid system successfully swapped off pieces down to the endgame. However, his opponent had a very active King and managed to grind out the win.

Geoff played a *Queen's Pawn, London System* and seemed to have a strong knight on c5, but his opponent created kingside pressure and sac'ed an exchange to get a strong attack.

Dave Dave played his normal *Dutch Defence*, and ended up with a slightly scary position where he could no longer castle. Although he managed to advance his kingside pawns and seemed to be doing OK, he was eventually ground down.

Dave the Power played his normal *Reti*. However, his opponent was worried that his own counter-attack would over-press, and offered a draw. Another half-point.

So another defeat for ECA. However, all is not lost, as we have yet to play some of the teams we would expect to beat. Next week is Holmes Chapel!

Postscript (TR):

Phil must have thought, but did not add, *Holmes Chapel is not one of the teams we expect to beat.*

Attacking Maniacs and Perfectionists

From: Tudor
To: Club members

An article in Chess World summarises five common styles of play, and how to deal with them. I was intrigued enough to allocate myself to one of these categories, then I guessed for a few other club members. No, I am not going to share these with you.

Here are the five styles, and hints at how to deal with them. Health warning: the descriptions are just preferred styles suggesting a player's comfort zone, not the only way anyone would be expected to act under all circumstances.

1. Attacking Maniac

Attacking maniacs go for attacks at all costs. They are chess players who prefer roulette. The best approach for playing against them is take your time, stay cool as you will usually find something they have missed.

2. Passive Player

They are complete opposites of the attacking maniacs. They only play low-risk moves. Beat them by mixing things up. They will avoid risky moves and will have to become more defensive.

3. Exchanger

This is a type of players that swops whenever possible. Their goal is to exchange as a strategy for avoiding a loss. But unlike stronger players they are not exchanging for advantage.

Exchange your passive/inferior pieces for their good/active pieces and win the endgame.

4. Perfectionist

This type of chess players is never satisfied with the moves they find. They get into bad time trouble. Capitalise on the time trouble these players will get themselves into.

5. Strategist

These chess players like planning everything That is not necessary a bad thing, if you're in trouble against this type of player, you should not worry about him simplifying a position for an easy win. His plans may not be calculable so you are never out of the game.

I favour style No 1, that of the desperate attacking maniac. It's not out of preference, but mainly because I often get into losing positions. I find creating complications that are hard to calculate is the best way to go from a possible loss to a win.

From: Dave Dave
To: All members

It took me about five seconds to allocate myself to one of the five groups, the Perfectionist, which is less time than I normally spend writing down my move, after the twenty-five minutes it takes me to decide which rook to move.

Doing a Leicester

From: T.R.
To: all members

Chess at East Cheadle is of prime importance to twenty or so members of the club, playing out of a sleepy corner of the North West of England.

More nationally, a far bigger sports story is brewing up. Last year, we had something common with the unfashionable football club, Leicester City.

We were both struggling to avoid relegation. We were both facing opposition far beyond our top players. We both had just managed to avoid the drop. We both were strengthened by new players. But from the start of the 1915-16 season, our fortunes have diverged.

Leicester's still unfancied players have begun with a bang, and shot the club to the top of the Premier League. Its distinguished manager Claudio Ranieri was primarily known for tinkering with his teams, and for being replaced twice at Chelsea, by the charismatic Jose Mourinho.

Irony of Ironies. I had been tracking the decline in Jose's fortunes as the season unfolded. By the time East Cheadle had compiled a disappointing first half of the Chess season, Jose's Chelsea was languishing as close to the bottom of the Premier league as was East Cheadle. Jose had been fired from Chelsea. The talent in Ranieri's team was becoming increasingly noticed.

Could they become giant killers? If so, could the fortunes of East Cheadle also be turned around? Our leadership team has retained the respect of the players, but I don't think I was alone in expecting our bad start might not be turned around.

Meanwhile, the sporting press were enjoying Leicester's success and the discomfort of its more prestigious rivals. Chelsea, of course, but also Manchester United, a shadow of the championship-winning teams under the great Sir Alex Ferguson a few seasons ago.

Enjoy it as long as it lasts. Former Leicester and England striker Gary Linacre is doing so in his role as BBC's chief pundit in its Match of the Day (MOTD) show. Week after week on the programme, he praises the brilliance of Leicester's Jamie Yardy, urging him for international selection.

But even Gary doesn't think that Leicester City will go on to win the league.

Many years earlier, a MOTD prediction about the emerging Manchester United team returned to haunt the inexperienced but hugely self-confident Alan Hansen. In 2005. United had lost the first match of the season to Aston Villa (coincidentally the bookie's favourite for relegation this year). 'You'll never win anything with kids', the former Liverpool and Scotland star famously said. He was so wrong.

Now, Gary made a similarly emphatic assertion. However much he would like it to be different, Leicester will not, cannot, win the title. They will eventually by outgunned by the Gunners, and far out-financed by Manchester City.

Indeed, Gary went on, if the impossible happened, and Leicester became title-holders, he will present

MOTD in his underwear. This is a promise he is being regularly reminded of, as the season progresses, while Leicester remain at the top of the table.

Here then, is my Linacre vow: If East Cheadle wins the first and second division championships, and at least one cup competition, I will write a book about our triumphs, and sign copies in the window of Simply Books, Bramhall, dressed as Grayson Perry

From: Dave Dave

To: T.R.

Not a pretty thought. Marginally better than Linacre giving free advertising to Marks and Spencer, by appearing on MOTD dressed only in a pair of M&S Boxer Shorts.

What Have they done to my Brain?

As emails zapped between club members, an increasing sense of gallows humour emerged. Steve sent me the following, which was intended as continuation of exchanges between Dave Dave and myself about attacking maniacs and time-troubled perfectionists. Having sent it, he worried it might be seen as cruel satire rather than a light-hearted continuation of the conversation.

From: Steve
To:Tudor

When I was recruited to East Cheadle recently through countless gifts and promises, my handler, who must remain anonymous of course, made it clear that my admission to the club would be subject to a meeting of the elders and an induction programme.

After several months I was invited to sit in on part - and only part - of some of these meetings. One thing I could never understand, was that any snippet of information remotely interesting always ended with the warning – "but don't tell Tudor!" [T.R.: Ironic reference to my compulsive reworking of material into blog posts or other written outputs]

I grew impatient and curious, until one day arriving early at the house of the grand elder, I happened upon the minutes of a previous meeting.

Anyway, what I read was surprising, although, in all the circumstances, understandable. It seems that in the 2013 season, it was noted by the elders that you were prone to 'attack exuberance'. This led you to lose interest during games where your attacks had become exhausted or where your opponent played mind-games with you (e.g. by playing the *Fort Knox* defence designed and developed by among others, Dave the Power for just such a purpose).

It was decided to insert a cranial chip during one of these 'interludes' - apparently this is easily done through the left ear with a syringe. The chip had a number of programmed options including an 'offer draw' mode and a 'resolute defence' mode, even in extremis, a *Petrosian* or no-mistake mode, as well as an 'attack' mode that would obviously not often be needed much in your case.

Anyway, shortly afterwards the chip began to malfunction. I believe - and I don't know the full story - that it somehow got stuck in attack mode, the very bias it was intended to inhibit. Since then there has been no opportunity to retrieve and re-programme the chip to meet the requirements of cautious defence and sometimes offering a draw when it might be risky to play on.

The elders decided that if reprogramming was not an option, then a solution of 'behavioural engineering' would need to be applied. The Grand Elder was a fan of the film *The Great Escape* and, as he is empowered to draw analogies from all life, he decided that a spell 'in the cooler' should sort you out. The blindfolding during your journey was unrelated and was designed to calm you down - a technique used by one of the elders when taking his dog to the vets.

I must stress I had no part in this. The role I was assigned was merely to agree a draw as quickly as possible and to observe you.

I have to say that my observations were mixed. I noted that you were resting your eyes from time, which I put down to the cooling effects. On the other hand, when you became fully engaged again I observed you jumped up shouting “attack, attack!” and on another occasion, “charge!”

It has been pointed out that my namesake Steve McQueen needed weeks on end in the cooler and even then his behaviour barely changed. Three hours is unlikely to sort the problem.

Anyway, Tudor, what I am really saying is it's all for your own good. With or without the chip, a period of draw-seeking moves would be in the interests and traditions of this grand old club.

Postscript [T.R.]: Steve had been influenced by my own light-hearted (I hoped) emails of our losses, such as the one about training sessions in a cryogenic chamber to prepare us for the winter conditions that prevail at some venues in the league.

He then sent a second message, hoping I had not been offended by his creative exuberance.

I hadn’t been.

Those Troublesome Time Controls Again

The winter break passed with a remarkable unilateral cease-fire by the weather Gods. Apart from the sneak attacks by sleet fighters, 2015 ended its soggy time without serious incursions into the pasture-lands of East Cheadle.

I was finishing off *Mourinho Matters* planning for its early release in the New Year.

Jose Mourinho had started the season at Chelsea with high hopes of further success for his team of thoroughbreds. It had ended in his dismissal. Not unlike East Cheadle Chess Club, I thought, although there won't be any dismissals. There are rarely enough willing members to take on the various onerous duties, among them those of the team captains.

On Christmas day, the Queen made her traditional speech to the nation. Its theme was *Light will Overcome Darkness*. I had mentioned it as an appropriate epilogue in *Mourinho Matters*. It also seemed appropriate to the future of East Cheadle chess club.

I turned my attention to the chess equivalent of the *angels on a pin* question, namely the matter of how long a chess game should last, and under what time system.

The time control in chess is a topic of endless debate. East Cheadle has its own particular problems with the recently introduced Fischer system of time control, which gives players an additional ten seconds after each move made. This has become possible as a result of electronic clocks.

The following messages on this important topic were sent 9-10 January 2016.

From: T.R.
To: Club members

Tough result. Well done Bill. Bad luck Dave.
Wonder what others think?
If we have choice of time control, the Fischer time limit of 1hr 20 mins plus 10 seconds each move added by the clock, is more friendly for players who get into time trouble. I prefer the 'no increment' 1 hr 30 mins to finish the game. It puts more time pressure on both players and we might get a few wins against stronger players
Over to you, captains and colleagues!

From: Dave Dave:
To: Club members

As always, Tudor is very thought provoking. As you all know, I often get into severe time trouble and do find Fischer time helpful from that point of view. I can say from experience that either is preferable to thinking you are playing Fischer and then discovering you aren't!

From: Jim
To: Club members

Hard luck guys - I think Dave was quite hard done by, in not getting a win in the circumstances but it would not have affected the team result. All in all, we put up a very good show against a strong team.

From: Edwin
To: Club members

I hate the +10 seconds (or anything of that kind) of the Fischer time control system. It adds an unnecessary complication in my view. The clock is supposed to add pressure if you have been taking too long.

Theoretically a game could go on forever with Fischer time. but in practice not. If 90 mins isn't long enough for the more “thoughtful” player, then make each game 105 mins instead. However, I suspect that players would still get into time trouble if they had 105 mins to make all their moves. After all, you only get into time trouble if you ignore the clock.

I watched Phil play someone a few years ago, with the +10 secs time rule, I can't remember where but very admirable. He let his clock run down to 1 second to go and quick as a flash made about a dozen moves as his opponent tried to capitalise on the limited time left. Suddenly he had only two minutes of time left, and his opponent had blundered.

I'm sure Phil did it deliberately to excite his opponent into a potential win on time, then deflate him with a series of hellishly good moves. So it can add also an extra dimension to play.

From: Phil

To: Edwin
cc Club members

That is very generous of you Edwin, to assume that my bad clock management was a deliberate strategy. Actually I think my brain got stuck and I only unstuck it with 2 seconds left.

It was in the Manchester rapid-play. It was a great game but fried my brain for the rest of the tournament. Just to prove my time management was not deliberate, I lost on time a few games later.

For the record I prefer the increments of Fischer time, as it avoids the "pieces flying all over the room" scenario when the clock gets really low.

From: Dave Dave
To: Club members

I can recall an even more famous game at the Ethiad stadium when, down to 2 minutes on the clock, my beloved City ... [unable to complete email, overcome by the memory].

From: Keven
To: Club members

This reminds me of another infamous incident of recent times when we had three Daves playing for us. Many will recall that one of the Davids (not Dave Dave) was a rook down, but his opponent was very short of time.

A 200+ player apparently stepped in and told the team-mate that he could claim a draw.

After which a row ensued, as Dave knew that the intervention was not from the team captain, the only one permitted to become involved. I cannot recall whether the blatant rule breaker, a well-known of near master-strength the 200+ was playing in the match or not. However, eventually the next day, after being lambasted by Dave, the opposition conceded the game.

Who says Chess is dull?

From: Paul
To: Club members

I missed the shootout we are discussing, but I did watch the end of that game played by Phil at the Ethiad. I think you were down to 2 seconds and then banged out a series of moves and were back up to over 2 minutes on your clock in a blink.

The advantage of the increments arrangement is that it also cuts out possible draw disputes with arbiters.

Incidentally, I lost a match with no increments, in the Blackpool quick-play this year in a mad scramble on time and when my opponent had about 10 seconds left. I was a piece up and he had no chance of a win. The arbiter happened to be watching our match and told me afterwards that I should have stopped the clock and claimed a draw.

The Fide rule is something like

"article 10 of the FIDE laws of chess states that when a player has less than two minutes on their clock they

may claim a draw if their opponent is not attempting to win the game by normal means. In other words, a draw is claimable if the opponent is merely attempting to win on time, or cannot possibly win except on time. It is up to the arbiter to decide whether such a claim will be granted or not."

I wasn't aware of this rule, but playing with an increment cuts all this out.

From: Ian
To: Club members

Hi folks. It would be illegal for the Captain or anyone else during the game to tell the player that he could claim a draw. The FIDE Rules state:

"During play the players are forbidden to make use of any notes, sources of information or advice, or analyse on another chessboard." (12.3 a.)

It's Not Just Us

From: Tudor
To: Club members

Regarding electronic clocks. It's not just us. A glance at the website of another club showed they had put the instructions for working their clocks on the site. I have pasted some of the information to show that our clocks are, in comparison, cuddly creatures. I have cut out at least 30% of additional notes going into finer detail of operating these chess monsters. But adding 10% as my own annotations.

The whole piece indicates that you need an IQ of near-genius level even to get the clocks working at Holmes Chapel:

Navigating the Clock

Use the joystick left and right to navigate between Modes 1 to 7, and move the joystick up and down to change the settings in each mode. Check the underneath of the clock to see what modes are available. Note, if you have selected Modes 3 or 7, you cannot move to other modes until you have navigated up or down to the setting with the — symbol.

[T.R.: Joystick? *On a Clock*? A team trying to set these clocks at the start of a match would be wonderful to behold, with clocks being turned upside down to see the modes, then back upright to check other things.]

Setting the clock for our leagues

We need two different settings for the Stoke league and one for the Stockport leagues. The three user-settings are set up as follows:

7A – Stockport League, from September 2012. All the moves in 90 minutes.

7B – Stoke League, Fischer timing. All the moves in 75 minutes, with ten seconds per move added before.

7C – Stoke league, old timing. All the moves in 85 minutes.

Playing with the clock

After switching on and navigating to 7A, 7B (looks like 78) or 7C, Black hits his button to start White's clock. If the clock needs to be stopped for any reason, press the Pause button. Restart the game by pressing the Pause button again. For a fresh game, hold down the Pause button to reset the clock.

If you don't like the beeps, or the lights, set the on/off button accordingly.

If someone has lost on time, both clocks start flashing and the player whose time is 0:00 has lost.

[Local knowledge: Mode 7B looks like 78]

Replacing the user settings

When the batteries expire and a new set (2 x C type) is inserted in a clock, the user settings disappear and will need to be re-programmed. Perhaps someone alters one of the user settings, and they need to be changed back. Here's how to do it:

The three user settings are set up by editing a pre-set mode and then storing it in one of the user settings, 7A, 7B and 7C, as follows:

[No, I would be gibbering at this stage, looking to see if we had any geniuses who seemed to know what was going on].

7A – Stockport League. All the moves in 90 minutes. Created by editing 2A.

7B – Stoke League, Fischer timing. All the moves in 75 minutes, with ten seconds per move added before. Created by editing 4A.

7C – Stoke league, old timing. All the moves in 85 minutes. Created by editing 2A.

[TR: A magnificent piece of technical writing.]

Mea Culpa

From: Bill
To: Club members

Hi all. Just seen the time trouble emails. Paul was very decent in not naming the culprit in all this. It was me.

I set the offending clock wrongly. The code for Fischer time is 3 which adds on the bonus seconds.

I apologised to everyone on the night and again afterwards to Dave and Paul who have been very gracious about it. For this, much thanks. I felt a right idiot.

It was so ironic because I won using a clock correctly set for Fischer time. As Paul mentioned, I was down to two seconds, one pawn ahead, when I deliberately moved my King into a discovered check position. I had a possible checkmate myself with my opponent's only defence being a queen exchange.

Despite having an escape square for my King, I chose a dodgy-looking move, hoping that my opponent would think I had made a mistake in time pressure. I tempted him into making an even bigger one.

So, apologies once more, and I vote for Fischer time.

Getting our Act Together

As the New year starts, members of East Cheadle's finest continue to exchange messages. While there were some efforts to discuss chess and how to win more games, the general tone is one of gallows humour.

Steve's reference to my recent talk at the club was particularly kind, as he is literally in a different league to myself, playing well above my rating in The Manchester league, as well as now appearing for East Cheadle in our Cheshire one.

I have edited out material that might be deemed inappropriate for a wider readership.

From: Stephen
To: Tudor

I was discussing last evening's games with John, and my time trouble, and I cast my mind back to your guidelines given in your lecture. The question I have is this:

When my opponent is spending a long time choosing his move amongst several options, I have difficulty in staying at the board analysing possible responses which may never see the light of day. Is this laziness or just brain energy conservation?

I would be very interested in knowing what my colleagues think about during these episodes. In last evening's game, instead of analysing the game itself during some of my opponent's long thinks, I found myself ruminating about the question:

I decided I should return to the board and look for *general themes* e.g. does he have multiple pieces that could be forked or skewered, or how might I get an opportunity to get my side-lined knight into play? In other words, engaging in small talk to myself instead of looking for a killer question.

So, I would be interested to know what other people think about when it is the other guy's move. Is it worth examining lines that won't happen or thinking about something else?

From: Tudor

To: Steve

I'm reading Kasparov's book *How Life Imitates Chess*. It discusses Analysis versus Intuition. Lots of great stuff. I won't attempt to paraphrase.

Taking your question, Kasparov touches on this, especially the chapter on the decision making process.

'Looking at five different options two moves deep is no better or worse than looking at only two options five moves deep, depending on the problem, the position, at hand' [p 160].

He also explores situations when calculation is more or less productive than trusting your intuition or judgement. His point is that sometimes you need to calculate, sometimes to trust your judgement.

Mid-Season High Spirits

I mentioned to Dave Dave that the creativity demonstrated in our e-mail exchanges could be turned into a film. Inevitably, it produced another burst of emails.

From: Dave Dave [sent by electronic tortoise]

Dear Mr Rickards,

I understand from my agent that you may soon be going into production with a new epic based loosely on a local Chess Club.

I wish to audition for the part of David the Super-Hero in this production. I possess the following super powers, which I believe make me perfect for the role.

a) I have enhanced vision which allows me to see through glass.

b) I am as fast as a slightly annoyed pensioner

c) I can speak eight different languages fluently...OK seven, well six really, five if you don't count Klingon. Yes, alright, I cheated in my CSE French; what do you mean Yorkshire doesn't count as a language?

From: T.R.
To: Dave Dave

Dear Dave, (if I may), or agent thereof,

The role as David super-hero has already been filled by a celebrity pensioner with experience of such films as

Shootout at the Fort Knox Corral, *The Great Fort Knox bullion heist*, and the TV family show *Opportunity Knox*.

We are still auditioning for a humorous role played by a village-idiot type character who gets amusingly confused over writing down the moves, which team he is playing for, setting electronic clocks and finding his way to Wilmslow chess club.

There are opportunities for 1,993 extras to complete our claimed cast of thousands.

We are also rather light on lighting technicians, and short on undersized players with a Welsh accent.

Please send your portfolio if you think you have the necessary life-experiences in any of these important roles in our ensemble.

Warmly yours in artistic integrity,

Alfred Spatchcock,
Director
Producer
Script writer
Dog trainer
First Grip
and Stand-in for superhero David in the cryogenic sequences.

The Seniors Prize

February 7 2016

The Dalai Lama sighed. His friend the Major had been loyal and supportive of East Cheadle since before the time of the great schism and the departure of West Cheadle to another league. He still seemed to influence the club through his generosity, although he has not visited in person for some years.

He looked at the hand-written sheet of proper writing paper, and the familiar and still unshaking handwriting. At least the AGM was several months away. Time to discuss what best to do with David and the other committee members.

Dear President,

I write on a formal matter. I request that you place it before the full meeting of the club at the next AGM.

It is my wish to provide a prize open to members of the club over the age of seventy. I need not remind you that you yourself would have been eligible for nearly a decade.

I have established that some eleven members would be eligible. I believe this would give them an additional motivation to attend club nights.

The only restriction I would place, is that competitors should attend following the dress code which was *de rigueur* when I was playing regularly, no more than fifteen years ago.

This, with adequate explanation on the club notice-board, would of course be an encouragement to younger members to do the same.

Perhaps you could let me know what fee would be appropriate for the club to be able to obtain a suitable trophy.

I will also make arrangements for funding for the inscription of the winner's name each year.

Sincerely,

Major Max

A Close Loss to the Big Macc by the A team

From: Phil
To: Club members

Macc A 3.5 ECA 2.5 - the boring details

If you haven't read Tudor's post reproduced elsewhere you really should. His travel story is a bit wild, but the bit about the icicles was only a slight exaggeration - the room really was frigid and the electric heater seemed to mainly be there for decoration.

Steve on board one played solidly as ever and when offered a draw by his master-strength opponent decided not to tempt fate.

I had a good opening with pressure against my opponent's centre. However, my opponent didn't make life easy for me and when he made a move I hadn't considered after I snatched a central pawn, I gave up to exchange. According to the computer I could have ended a clear pawn up. I had some slight pressure for the exchange but some rather wild moves in time pressure meant I ended up a Rook down. Sigh.

John, as white, found himself in uncharted territories before getting back into a line he knew well. He got a very comfortable endgame where his opponent's two remaining pieces were stymied. Despite the shock of realising there was no time control, John held it together and his opponent ended up losing on time. [John had wrongly assumed that there would be a 'reset' of clocks at some point, and nearly lost. This is an example of an on-going debate about time controls by John and other club members.]

Geoff played his favourite *Owen's Defence*, which is coming into favour, with its hypermodern fianchettoed queen's bishop giving tactical chances in the centre and king's side. Geoff castled 'long' behind the bishop and won material with a strong attack. A great win for Geoff.

Tudor played a pawn rush as White. His opponent seemed to be familiar with the system and defended well as well as counter-attacking against Tudor's queenside king.

Fort Knox David played his favourite system but the fort was compromised and he lost a pawn and then the endgame.

So eventually Macclesfield's strength in depth told and we lost narrowly but put up a great fight.

Considering the grade deficit, it was a great effort and almost another point. I have a feeling our first win isn't far away!

Postscript [T.R.]:

Phil has become as optimistic as Paul about our chances for the remainder of the season. I am not so sure.

The Moment of Truth

Phil and his wife were making their way back to the car park of the Parrswood entertainment centre in Didsbury. They had been to see *The Bridge of Spies* at the Cineworld multiplex, and were still discussing the brilliant performances of Tom Hanks and Garry Rylance as they crossed in front of the casino and bowling alley.

A chilly February wind was whipping up debris and mingling the aroma of popcorn with that of the grilled offerings coming from Franky and Benny's and the Chiquito Restaurant Bar & Mexican Grill.

Even in the semi-darkness, he recognised Paul's over-sized car parked next to him, squeezed into an under-sized parking space.

Phil was about to break his promise of no chess talk on their visits to the cinema. The tinted window of the car slid down and Paul's cheerful face appeared.

It was not a night for long discussions. Phil introduced his wife, and they scrambled into their own car, grateful to escape the Manchester drizzle. Before driving off, and across opened windows, the two chess players and their partners chatted briefly about how much they had enjoyed the film.

Then, almost automatically, Phil began a parting conversation about the critical state of affairs at East Cheadle regarding demotion prospects.

"We need someone like Tom Hanks to rescue the first team this time" he said. "It would take Houdini to help us escape from this"

Paul was smiling wryly as he cautiously backed his car out of the space. "Make that a Double Houdini" he replied.

The windows closed, and Paul drove off.

A cavorting crisp-packet blew across the windscreen of Phil's car before attaching itself beneath his wiper like an airborne parking ticket.

A Breathtakingly Beautiful Breakthrough by the B Team

From: Paul
To: all members

ECB 3.5 - 2.5 Altrincham A

Yes, you read that right. We managed to pull off our first win of the season but it wasn't altogether straightforward! Halfway through the night we looked like we were cruising. But we made hard work of it before getting the right result in the end.

Nick finished first on board 5. He was a pawn up for a long time but ended up in a very equal -looking position for a draw.

According to *Fritz*, I was leading overwhelmingly (plus 13.5, which is computer-speak for *why doesn't he resign?*) I then contrived to lose a game when I was a full piece up by allowed my opponent a sucker punch sneaking down my a-file.

Dave the Power was in a tight battle of two rooks each plus pawns. David's five pawns were all connected but his opponent had two troublesome although unconnected past pawns. David finally agreed a draw after about the fifth request.

Tudor went two pawns up in an opposite colour bishop ending and was able to use the principle of two weaknesses to overwork his opponent's bishop for a nice win.

Meanwhile Geoff was a pawn up with a passed pawn but was just unable to make any progress and agreed a valuable draw.

So it was two and a half points each, with the whole match to be decided by board 1.

Dave Dave, the king of time trouble, was having another clock horror. He was a pawn down in a Q and R endgame but had good pressure along the 7th rank. Dave ran his clock down to 1 second (!) (The Fischer time system again) and made a couple of quick moves before offering a draw.

His opponent, perhaps caught up in Dave's time scramble, played on, but made a soft move which let Dave in on the back rank and he was able to very efficiently weave a mating net with Q and R for a last gasp winner.

As they say in other sports, now we have to keep up the momentum.

Well done us.

Chess in a Cold Climate

Cap'n Phil's account of our A team match against Macclesfield did not do justice to the extreme weather conditions we suffered. I decided to offer an alternative account.

From: Tudor
To: all members

You never know what might happen in any chess game. Following the triumph of my *don't make these mistakes* presentation, I offer another hard-learned lesson from a recent bruising encounter with the Big Macc's A team.

Discovering that I was down to play was arguably my first blunder. I had ignored an earlier message from Captain Phil asking for my assistance, due to the late withdrawal of one of his original picks (*I know who you are, you wimp. A golden wedding anniversary is an inadequate excuse when we are chasing our first point of the season*).

My attempt to avoid the match was in vain. I was press- ganged into a car at night and driven via a complex route by the driver known as Fort Knox Dave or Dave the Power for some reason.

We picked up an accomplice of his somewhere to the south of Carlisle, and then doubled back to the Steppes of Macclesfield.

I was hustled to the imposing entrance hall of Macclesfield Liberals club, where my blindfold and handcuffs were removed. I was told I would be abandoned to my fate there if I did not cooperate and join the other conscripts.

I suspected something was wrong when I noting the icicles hanging from the mighty entrance gate. I was roughly manhandled up several flights of unlit stairs and pushed into a dimly lit room. Eventually assorted unkempt and shivering individuals shuffled in. Some set about moving ancient tables together and setting up chess boards and clocks. Others huddled together, whimpering with the cold around the puny heater which did not seem to be working.

You will not learn any of this from the heavily redacted version on the ECC official website. Oh, no.

We were saved from a painful death by freezing only because another consignment of pressed men was pushed roughly into the room, adding somewhat to the ambient temperature and the scent of nervous creatures fearing what they were about to face.

And so I played, compliant to the wishes of Captain Phil and his henchmen.

The great warriors of Macclesfield were about to savage their latest victims. One of our number, known as Big John was determined to take down his mighty opponent, suckering him into a time-trouble trick he had learned from Brother Dave Dave.

Another, Brother Geoff, wounded and finished off his opponent, and then Brother Stephen fought to a standstill securing an honourable draw.

I draw a veil over the losses suffered by Captain Phil and Dave the Power.

ECC could still achieve a miraculous victory if I could only, er, what is it called, win.

But I couldn't.

I couldn't even draw.

My captors returned me to my home in silence. I was only marginally suffering physically. The frostbite is not requiring surgery, but the mental scars remain.

A Point, a Point, my Kingdom for a Point!

Shortly after the B team's first victory, Phil posted the much awaited news of a point gained by the A team, and against strong opposition. He gave me even more pause to question my own approach to chess:

ECA 3 Holmes Chapel 3

A point, a point, my kingdom for a point! ECA finally got off the mark last night with a fine draw away to Holmes Chapel. If it hadn't been for my brain seizure in the final minutes it could have been more ...

Steve played a *King's Indian Attack*, and a complicated game ensued. This white opening has some of the features of the more common *King's Indian Defence* played as black. His opponent found his way through a maze of complications to a draw.

My opponent (another Geoff) played his favourite *Owen's Defence* but came unstuck in the middle-game and lost two pawns. It looked hopeless but Geoff got an active Bishop against a slightly stranded Knight and managed to win the pawns back. A fantastic fighting draw.

My opponent played a bit of a side-line against my King's Indian (defence this time, as black) and I responded in an unusual way leaving us both in the dark. I was allowed to establish strong centre pawns but most of the pieces came off and my opponent offered me a draw. I decided that I liked my position and played on.

Then after a few more exchanges I decided that I had nothing and offered a draw. This time my opponent declined, but allowed me to push my central pawns and ended up having to give up a piece to stop them. So I was a piece up in a Queen ending but with my clock ticking down I couldn't work out how best to win and my opponent found a perpetual check.

John won stylishly. It is a brave man who allows John his favourite *Queen's Gambit.* John established a Knight in the centre and pushed his Kingside pawns with a fine crushing attack. A great win for John.

Geoff played his favourite *Owen's Defence*, the subject of his club-night exposition. He has a great way of pressuring white with his bishop on the b7 square and kingside tactics.

But tonight he came unstuck in the middle-game and lost two pawns. It looked hopeless but Geoff got an active Bishop against a slightly stranded Knight and managed to win the pawns back. A fantastic fighting draw.

David played an *English Opening* and always seemed to have a nicer position with queenside pressure and his opponent having a very bad Bishop. A very solid draw from our *Fort Knox* Drawmeister.

The *Alekhine's Defence* can be risky, and Tudor was unable to create his usual complications to escape from a bind.

Overall a great result considering we were heavily out-graded on the bottom boards. This point could be crucial at the end of the season, if our matches against Denton and Chorlton cancel themselves out.

`From: Tudor
To: All members

I am in denial about giving up on the Alekhine, my one and only defence against white's king pawn opening. I have no appetite for studying the other options I have tried and given up on over the years.

Phil is probably right, and I should at least make an effort. I don't play in tournaments anymore. I haven't even recruited a Serbian coach (although Geoff does his best, when free on a Thursday afternoon. His *Stonewall Defence* is a work of art).

Maybe there is a deeper psychological explanation. Perhaps I want to cling on to the delusional belief that I really could do better, if only I had time for tournaments, Serbian coaches, and opening study.

The Ocular Proof

I have visited opticians since I was very young. The earliest I remember was a Mr Gilbert Tritcheler, who practiced in Pontypridd, the nearest town to the little village where I was growing up.

He was very tall, very thin, and had a pointed beard which made him look a bit like photographs I had seen of Sigmund Freud.

I set out to impress him, but he was a hard man to impress, rightly seeing me as more than a bit precocious. He provided me with my first set of specs, and perhaps influenced my intention to grow a beard as quickly as biologically possible.

Since then, I have moved and acquired various opticians in the process. I still own a wonderful pair of tinted sports spectacles in a metal case, a consequence of an accident to my existing pair of working specs on a visit to Singapore. Someone from a local Mall rustled up the replacements in twenty-four hours.

Over the last ten years, I have remained loyal to a local practice, resisting the blandishments coming from the brilliant series of Specsavers advertisements. (I particularly like the one about the myopic vet desperately attempting to revive his assistant's fluffy hat.)

The service has been fine, although my attendance has been rather desultory. At first, I found some dark humour in the surgery which was on the first floor up a narrow staircase that must have been a struggle for patients. Reaching the summit, there was one last obstacle to be negotiated. A low wooden beam, above which in very large letters (what else?) the injunction *Mind the step*.

Five years ago I had been warned that I might need cataract surgery in the right eye. This proved to be the case, and I eventually received brilliant remedial treatment. The main recovery problem was the month in which multiple eye drops had to be applied. The surgeon warned me that I might one day have to consider a similar procedure.

The optician reinforced the warning of two years ago. I had no doubt that he would now find my left eye to be in need of similar treatment.

After the examination, he searched for the best opening gambit. He chose the left flank opening.

"The left eye is a lot worse …"

It was my move. Would I play a solid Fort Knox like defence to postpone the inevitable? I had procrastinated in starting this particular game, but with Coach David's warning at tennis, my mind was already made up.

"Let's get it done" I said.

"Better before the summer" he continued. "Don't want too much glare from the sun afterwards."

I was thinking of changed holiday plans. I was also thinking of how it might influence the small part I might be able to play in the fortunes of the East Cheadle Chess A and B teams.

The Apotheosis of Sir Stephen

From: Phil

To all members
ECA 2.5 Marple A 3.5

The match between our A team and Marple A took place yesterday. The outcome hinged on Steve's game at the end, with both players on less than 5 minutes. Steve had a Q & K against his master-strength opponent. The whole club and visitors gathered around and watched for at least 10-15 minutes as Steve tried his best, but brilliant play resulted in a draw.

Tudor has supplied a version of events below. He has invented even more names for our team members, but I think they are easy enough to work out who is who.

From: Tudor
To: all members

Annus Mirabilis: The Apotheosis of Sir Stephen

I tell of great deeds of courage and skill in battle. The knights of the East Cheadle Round Table set out courageously for the mountains of Marple.

None battled more valiantly than Sir Stephen, against the young champion of Marple, Fernandez the fearsome. The other knights fought against the well trained opponents Even the skills of Sir John of Gascony who bore the coat of arms of the noble order of Reed

Warblers on his shield, were to no avail and he retired from the fray, swiftly followed by Sir David of Elmsmead Fort.

After many an hour in grim conditions, matching only those of the dank chambers of Chorlton, Sir Geoffrey Bristle agreed an honourable tie.

The aging celtic knight Sir Tudor Treforest launched a reckless attack which confused his youthful opponent, already disconcerted with attacking grunts from Sir T partly due to ingestion of a secret Welsh beverage quaffed throughout the contest. (*Ross on Wyan brew*).

A hit, a palpable hit, and East Cheshire were still in the contest.

The tourney was lost after Sir William, clad in his famous vermillion battledress, was thwarted and agreed a tied contest.

But all this while, as midnight approached, Sir Steven was engaged in battle against Fernandez the fearsome.

The field was strewn with the *hors de combat* fallen. The entire pawn army of each had gone, but the last one was ennobled to queen status, as Fernandez saw a brilliant defence. He fought on, now with a castle against Sir Steven's queen.

The task is a rare finale to a joust. According to the books of battle, the queen will prevail but unless you know the ancient lore, you may exceed the fifty move limit on hostilities.

The battle waged around all sixty-four chequered regions of the field. A crowd of hushed onlookers surrounded the combatants. Sir Steven pressed, and the queen could win the rook. Bur Fernandez had seen one move further, and taking the rook would but leave to a stalemate.

That was enough to take the contest to fifty moves without a capture, and thus deemed a draw.

The crowd erupted into a spontaneous round of applause.

The East Cheshire knights were defeated closely and honourably, but Sir Stephen had fought the young Marple champion to a standstill.

Crying over Spilt Drink

It could have been Red Bull, although it wasn’t. Other brands are also available. Or even one of the energy drinks you buy in tins on-line as a floury-looking powder which you dissolve in water.

I buy mine regularly, usually on the morning before a match, a small bottle of orange liquid. Usually I pick it up from Budgeons, my nearest convenience store, the only one on our High Street in the village of Woodford, a few miles to the south of East Cheadle as the rook flies.

I hesitate to mention a specific brand. Mine is to be found among a range of garishly-coloured fluorescent drinks, placed just out of the grasp of passing kiddiewinks in their buggies.

It is my drink of choice, intended to reduce those blunders I have started making a few hours after the start of a match.

Last night, it didn't just keep me mentally alert, even buzzily-wired. It almost wrecked the entire match. With different opponents, an objection to what happened may already have been submitted to the league complaints sub-committee, accompanied by statements from Paul and the opposing team captain.

I have mentioned the cramped circumstances found at some venues. This was among the most constricted, not unlike the one where I had lost after knocking over my pieces and touching the wrong bishop.

It would have been an uncomfortable squeeze, even without my bottle of energy drink. I had to sacrifice something from the table-top, so my drink was positioned under the table, to be reached for me to unscrew its bright red cap as needed.

This I did with care, avoiding spillage of liquid over the pieces of the game.

Nearly an hour after the start of the match, and we were well into a middle-game. My scoresheet showed we had made twenty moves. Across the table I could see the rival score sheet was closer to the bottom of its first column. I must have forgotten to record a few of the moves, so I wrote down the last few on the sheet again, to catch up.

I was well ahead on the clock. To my left, Dave the Power was proceeding at a more sedate pace, with about half as many moves played. I had no doubt that Dave Dave, seated to Dave the Power's left from my position, had made even fewer moves.

You might say that the system was existing in a state of fragile equilibrium, which might collapse into a more stable state of randomness by the fluttering wings of a butterfly off the west coast of America.

Well it might have been the butterfly, but the proximal agency was my shaking hand taking a swig out of the opened bottle.

The bottle fell on my board, scattering the pieces as in a mortar attack, and spraying its fizzy contents rather more widely.

With an involuntary action, Dave the Power, who had been leaning forward, disappeared under his table, dislodging his board. In a slow-motion domino effect, the neighbouring games also copped some fizzy spray.

It was at this moment of confusion when Paul showed his brilliant leadership skills.

“Stop the clocks” he cried. “Match suspended until we sort this out.”

Which is what we started to do, except for board six, which was positioned a little away from the other five boards, and whose players had been concentrating so hard, they had not heard Paul's orders.

I can now confirm that a few millilitres of 12% glucose solution propelled with force can spread a lot of stickiness. Much seemed to have found its way onto Dave the Power's head and shoulders. Other players were trying to remove viscous films from their spectacles and hearing aids.

But it was the chess pieces and boards that were the hardest to clean. We had to use the entire stock of toilet paper from the public loos downstairs to get the pieces fit for purpose and restart the games from agreed final positions.

Did we win the match? The records will show we didn't, and that the splattered players agreed rather quickly to draws on boards one to five. The unaffected home player on board six played a blinder, and his Anti-Hellespont defence won him the game, and resulted in a narrow defeat for East Cheadle, whose players went off to take a much-needed early bath.

I have decided to find a different drink, one with a non-spill delivery system, for future matches.

ECA Manage First Win of Season. Is it too late?

From: Phil
To: Club members

ECA 3.5 Denton A 2.5

Well I never. ECA managed a first win of the season last night against fellow strugglers Denton A. We managed to field our strongest team, and our strength in depth told in the end.

Steve played a solid *Ruy Lopez* one of the oldest of openings still in serious play. His opponent played well and after a number of exchanges had a slight initiative. However, she also had very little time left and Steve managed to create problems. Eventually he got his rook and queen behind her king with a mating attack.

As normal, I got a decent position out of the opening. In a variation of the hyper-accelerated *Sicilian Dragon* I am very familiar with, I had some pressure against my opponent's centre. I then tried to be clever rather than play an obvious recapture which left the position dead equal. In the complications I missed a simple threat to trap my knight.

Oh dear. I got a pawn for the piece and managed to create some pressure in the endgame but my opponent played solidly enough and held out for the win.

John faced a kind of *Nimzo-Indian* and was under pressure all over the board. He entered an endgame a couple of pawns down, but hung on with some help from the time control.

Kieran seemed to be doing OK in Geoff's recommended *Owen's Defence* but was behind in development. He then lost a pawn and the endgame.

Geoff played his favourite *Colle System* and got a strong knight on e5. He then advanced his central pawns for a smooth win.

Dave Dave's opponent did not manage to create many threats against his familiar *Accelerated Dragon*, and Dave smoothly outplayed his opponent, mating him in the endgame to win the match for us.

So we know now who are the relegation candidates. Although we are now two points behind Denton we have a match in hand. Things could still get interesting!

Postscript [TR]

Well done everyone. The A team draws level with the B team on matches won (one each). There is no doubt we are underdogs in most matches, based on individual grades. Phil is hinting that the A team may still struggle to pick up a few wins to avoid relegation. But there were even worse problems he was shortly to learn about.

Oh what can ail thee, Knight at arms?

Paul must have thought all the troubles of the season were worthwhile with the win for the A team. There was even the chance that results would go the way of East Cheadle.

Things hadn't worked out as he had hoped at the start of the season, but he had been right that the team would be strengthened by the arrival of Geoff and Steve. There had been an unusual series of accidents, without which they would surely have edged ahead of the other demotion candidates.

He knew the remaining fixtures by heart. One in particular, against Denton was a possible if he could field his strongest team.

Then another series of cruel blows. John sent a good luck email from France where he had decided to stay for a tournament. Keiran was again unavailable. But something Steve had said after the match had stuck in his memory.

"Is it true" Steve asked him "we are having to leave the Memorial Hall next year?"

Phil couldn't understand where Steve had got that idea from. "No, it's not true. Nothing's been decided but we would have heard from the Trust if there was any problem."

Steve shook his head. "I must have misunderstood. I was with Geoff playing in a County match over the weekend. We were both chatting with someone who mentioned it."

“Whoever it was got it wrong” Phil said. “Who was saying that we were moving?”

Steve looked rather guilty. “It was someone who said he used to play here.”

Phil guessed what was happening, and it was not good. It was Gladstone Whithers. If he had stayed with them, East Cheadle would certainly have been strong enough to stay up. Now he was trying to poach his best players.

“I don’t suppose he suggested you and Geoff could always be guaranteed a place in any team in the league?”

“Not really. He did say they kept open throughout the year, and we might like to play for them in the summer league. He knew that we close down then.”

“Sunderland” Phil muttered to himself.

Sunderland, even with their own Houdini-like manager Sam Allerdyce, were going through their annual fight to stay in the football premiership. It was only a matter of time. Then, once relegated, their few strongest players would be cherry-picked by other teams with promise of continued Premiership play. East Cheshire had more to lose than their place in the first division of their league.

Phil wondered how long it would be into the summer season before the wretched Whithers would make Steve, Geoff, and maybe John an offer they would be unable to refuse.

The Mysterious Nature of Reality

I came across an interesting article in this week's *Mid Lancashire Mercury*. It was written by Susie Yup, one of the paper's liveliest young reporters. Both she and her partner John Keane play for the *Post-modernists*, the reincarnation of the West Cheadle club, now in the Mid Lancashire chess league.

East Cheadle is due to play a friendly match at Urmston University shortly, in which John Keane is likely to be playing, maybe against our own East Cheadle John.

I was also interested in the article as someone who has been influenced by the work of an author I admire:

Susie Yup
Mid Lancashire Mercury

American novelist receives award from Urmston University

The distinguished novelist Paul Auster America visited Urmston University yesterday to receive an honorary degree. He was presented with a Doctorate by the Vice-Chancellor, Professor Wendy Lockinge for his services to literature.

Professor Lockinge said that Dr Auster has gained world-wide acclaim for his work which combines crime fiction, and the search for identity and personal meaning. The Vice-Chancellor explained how much she had been looking forward to meeting him, particularly because of her earlier experiences as a senior detective.

In receiving his award, Dr Auster replied

"I believe the world is filled with strange events. Reality is a great deal more mysterious than we ever give it credit for. My work has been attributed to various schools of thought such as post-modernism. I have to confess that I don't understand much of the work of the post-modern philosophers."

Dr Auster, who lives in Brookyn, New York, is the best-selling author of *The Invention of Solitude*, and *The New York Trilogy*, an award-winning series of literary detective stories in which the author appears in a baffling way.

Another Weird Way of Losing

From: Tudor
To: Club members
Report from Stockport Quick Play

I pause from striking my head against the dashboard and take out my iPad to report to ECC HQ.

It is 5.30 pm on a blustery Sunday afternoon in Greater Manchester.

Three hundred yards up the sodden A6, chess players are pouring out of the Davenport Arms, Stockport. Pouring is an apt word to describe conditions here. *Plentiful convenient parking* as on its website is more of a euphemism.

Making this report prevents me from further self-harm.

Why the lack of a stiff upper lip? Read on and maybe you will understand. I was taking part in the modest level of the Intermediate tournament, populated by many friends from the third division of the Stockport league, some even from the lofty reaches of the second division occupied by our B team.

Half way through the day, I was pleasantly surprised to be leading the field with 3 out of 3. Although a bit of a blur, my results are helped by opponents playing even more like attacking maniacs than myself, getting their recklessness in first.

So to lunch. I battle though a typhoon to reach the car and extract a nutritious banana. I return, dripping, into the arena. My opponent awaits. I try an opening suggestion for White from my new guru Mahatma Geoff. It seems to be working. I get a slight plus and long castling, tucking my king in safety. An attack is only a move or so away.

PAUSE WHILE I STRIKE THE DASHBOARD A FEW MORE TIMES.

But crassness is also not far away. He appears to block my attack with a temporary foray by a knight. I ignore it. Only to hear my opponent say that I had ignored a check. He seemed uncertain of the rules of the tournament and and asked what he should do?

I helpfully say that as I had made an illegal move, he can choose the piece I must move next.

THIS IS STUPIDLY WRONG.

It takes him a microsecond to suggest I sacrifice my queen, rather than the King move that leaves him in some difficulties.

I resign. Later I learn that the correct penalty was a bonus two minutes added to his clock, which would still have left him behind in time and weaker on the board.

I deservedly lost the next game, only to rally and outperform the other Over 60s to earn a consolation prize. Some consolation.

Not asking for sympathy. Is raw steak still considered good for a bruised face and ego?

A Dentonite Explosion

From: Paul
To: Club members

ECB Wins a Second Game

Denton B 1.5 - 4.5 ECB

Denton were playing 3 matches last night which meant we were up against a weakened team which enabled us to record our second successive win (a rarity!) As usual, it wasn't entirely straightforward.

Bill was first to finish in a fairly quick game. He was up against a *Scandinavian* (defence, not someone from Sweden). He handled it well, winning material and the game, before jogging home.

Keven was coasting in his game too and was the exchange up. Unfortunately, (and we've all done it) he was busy thinking about his next move and neglected the fact that his Queen was *en prise*.

Tudor was firing out the moves with his *Alekhine Defence*, and promoted a passed pawn to settle things.

David the Power was having a little trouble and was a pawn down before he managed to find a way of convincing his opponent that it was perpetual check.

Meanwhile Dave Dave, now obviously cured of his previous time issues, actually did the unthinkable - he won on time! He put his opponent in trouble with a variety of threats for a nice win.

In the B team, we normally have an *incident* and last night it was in my game. My opponent had clearly decided to park the bus, and by about move fifteen, although he had castled, all his other pieces had returned to their original starting squares!

My pieces were all active so I thought a sacrifice was in order to blow away his kingside. I went for a combination but it self-destructed. At the end of it I was the exchange up but had only three pieces to his five. Luckily he was struggling to coordinate his pieces and I managed to block his queen totally out the game in a corner. I started clawing back material and was almost level heading into a time scramble.

On the old-fashioned clocks available, I had about six minutes to his four, when he made a move - and forgot to hit his clock!

I milked it a bit with much head-scratching and chin stroking, making out that I was pondering over a move of huge complexity. This charade lasted for about 3 and a half minutes until he looked at the clock closely and - in horror - realised I had been stealing his time.

We played out a few more moves before I sheepishly pointed out that his flag had fallen. A very scruffy win for me and I really felt for him, particularly as the same thing has happened to me in the past and I know how bad it feels.

So all in all a good result, which puts us in a very healthy mid-table position.

Tudor's verdict is below.

As per Tudor:

Denton and the Time Lords

A great performance from the ECB team. I relinquish my dubious title of East Cheadle's Houdini either to captain Paul or to Dave Dave (leave anonymous voting slips in the dead-letter drop box in the Memorial Hall).

Paul as predator toyed with his unsuspecting prey, a veritable Cheetah against a Wildebeest. He gives up two pieces in anticipation of a Zugswang thirty moves later (or maybe not). The plan is working to perfection. The wildebeest is losing the will to escape its languid attacker.

Then a shift of plan, and a dazzling set of '*if he does that I do that*' and the wildebeest had collected a motley array of forces in exchange for a queen.

But the effort had brought the poor creature to a terminal state with insufficient energy to reach a paw out to stop his ticker from expiring. The Cheadle Cheetah watched as seconds ticked on to the last syllables of recorded time. Death was ultimately quiet and dignified.

Dave Dave, himself prone to time yips, was also in regal form. This time, his opponent did remember to press his clock at the conclusion of every move, but it was insufficient. Deadly Dave posed incalculable threats until the Denton top board sat helpless unable to decide whether to move, throw himself to the ground Eden Hazard fashion, or take an early bath.

Meanwhile Doc Tait had carried out a neat bit of keyhole surgery and went off to support the junior doctors.

The Governor, Dave the Power, grabbed a perpetual check that wasn't. The Denton second board had a blind spot showing he could have sneaked his king away to safety.

To my left, old sea dog Captain Birdseye Kev was involved in a skirmish which seemed very promising until he overlooked a sneak attack which shivered his timbers and pirated away his queen. 'I never saw it coming' said Kev ruefully.

Which leaves me, black, playing the *Alekhine Defence* (ignoring gentle hints from first team captain Phil about its general garbage-like qualities). White can completely neutralize black's chances by giving up all chances of winning. Then Black can spend a happy three hours in a dead parrot situation seeing if something might turn up.

My main danger was falling asleep. About sixty moves later I had a solitary pawn that gradually advanced and to the surprise of my opponent and myself became more and more likely to reach its destination, flopping down exhausted on the back rank, where it was transformed into a fully- grown queen.

So it was a victory.

As Doc Bill put it, no one beats East Cheadle B nineteen times in succession.

Two Points of View

My focus on the survival battles of the first and second teams means I have not noticed the glorious enthusiasm displayed, as well as good results, by our third and fourth teams.

East Cheadle C has more than held its own in the division. As ever, the strength of Macclesfield club extends through all three divisions in the league. I came across a nice example in the reports of the match played between East Cheadle C team and Macclesfield C towards the end of the season. I say reports, because I was able to track down two descriptions published as blogposts on the club websites.

It turns out that each club had a celebrity journalist embedded into its C team. Here are the chronicles of a tight contest, first from Edwin, who is sharing the C team leadership load with Myles, and then from Macclesfield's Hat Man Rickie. The names were dreamed up by Edwin for this particular match, and I have borrowed them for the Macclesfield account to make for easier comparisons.

Although Edwin gave himself the name the Fortunate, I think of him as Edwin the Enlightened, for his advanced skills with the mysteries of Information Technology. In his account he starts with the result and game scores, then gives an extended version of the match as it unfolds. Then Hatman Rickie offers a second perspective.

East Cheadle C Battles with Title Contenders Macclesfield C [Edwin's account]

We entertained the formidable Macclesfield C team last night, with the following result:

Paul the Dasher 0: Marc o'Polo1

Edwin The Fortunate 1: Hat Man Rickie 0

Ian The Draw Tiger ½: Dave Magnum Forced Draw 1/2

Keith The Draw Lion ½: Tom 'Robbo' The Draw Bridge1/2

Geoff The Not Draw 0: David The Stylish 1

Result: ECC 2 Macc C 3

Early doors, Paul the Dasher, our mercenary but welcomed conscript from ECB, was doing okay on board one against the fearsome Marc o'Polo, as was I, on board 2.

Ian The Draw Tiger and Keith The Draw Lion were looking slightly down on boards three and four. Geoff The Not Draw, was about even, as far as I could see, on board five. It all looked promising and it seemed that a draw was probably on.

Paul reported thus on his top board match:

'I succumbed to that old chestnut "*The Sniper Botvinnik* variation". [TR: I had never heard of this exotic opening, until my good friend Mr Google filled me in about it. A very unusual move order for white which with straightforward play gets into more conventional openings such as the English, which is itself a version of Dave Dave's *Sicilian played with the white pieces*. The sniper is our old friend a fianchettoed black square bishop, this time taking aim from behind the white army's lines].

At one stage, when I was well and truly sniped, my opponent Marc o' Polo had used four minutes on the clock and I had used an hour!

He knew the system well, and had been well booked and videoed on it but told me afterwards that I was actually coming up with a fairly main line defence and was in with a shout, before I made a mistake.'

Then Geoff The Not Draw came to an untimely fate, and the outlook looked bleak. 2-0 to Macc. There might be a possible whitewash on the cards.

However, Ian rallied to get in a drawing position, and Keith grabbed a knight with ease to hold a considerable material advantage.

With me in the ascendancy, as I will shortly turn to, ECC might still get something. I feel I have to report this game more fully, as I spent most time involved in it. [TR: And also because you won in somewhat Houdini fashion.]

I had arrived late, and was already five minutes down on the clock. Not to worry I thought. Then I saw that my opponent was the distinguished chess reporter Hit Man

Rickie, complete with back hat. His grade was a lot higher than mine at 128. Oh dear. I decided to play as tight as I could, defend and try to not make any mistakes. I played my currently favoured *The Queen's Sardines Gambit* [TR: This time it surely must be irony from Edwin].

My unusual attack is one where I start with a *Queens Gambit* then simply put as many pieces as I can into the four by four square territory fighting area square marked c1, c4, f1, f4. This has been working well this season. The game plodded on in a very dour manner, with my opponent adopting a *Kings Indian Defence*. Slowly the game unfolded with the words of Mithrandir playing in my head at the exit of Moria, "Though shalt not pass!".

I avoided any exchange of pieces, keeping my pawn line intact and finally succumbed as my opponent swapped white square bishops on move twelve. By this time, my knights had moved hobbit-like across to the right of the board and with little option for my opponent to move his pieces.

I sensed momentum building. Saying farewell to Tolkien, and returning to the tinned fish metaphor, I raised my key forged in the furnaces of Mordor, and started to roll back the lid on my sardine tin. This exposing both my king and his king, but to my advantage. I could quickly call up support from my queen, rooks and remaining bishop. Things were looking good. He was on the toast ready to go under the grill, when in a move the Marquis de Laissez-Faire would have been proud of …

…I gave my queen away. [TR: That's my kind of blunder.] Damn! I was down two rooks and a knight versus queen, rook and knight and equal on pawns. I was surely done for! I played on hoping my position was strong enough and I might get a lucky fork to grab his queen. [T.R.: I sense a Houdini escape coming up]. His prowess came to the fore and before long he had pinned my knight and was in a simple winning position.

All I had left was subterfuge. With one of my knights under attack, I played my rook along the back row to the h file. It would be checkmate if I had two consecutive moves. Oh for such luxury! [TR: This is the *oh for two consecutive moves* syndrome. Edwin has nothing to lose.]

However, it worked. It diverted his attention, and instead of swiping my knight and rolling on to a comfortable win, he pushed his pawn to give him a way out of the checkmate (that would never have been, if he simply took my knight).

I couldn't believe it, I had a chance, I pushed the rook to check. His king had only one move and there was now a serious danger he would either lose his bishop or queen and we could be level on points, but with me in a commanding position. He moved his king to the back row and I saw my chance, another shrewd check avoiding the obvious swap meant it was mate in one or two moves.

My sardines on toast were done! So I somehow managed to win.

With Ian The Draw Tiger forcing/agreeing a draw for the team, the hope was Keith The Draw Lion could press home his advantage against Tom 'Robbo' The Draw Bridge and salvage a draw for the C team.

In a tense finish and down on time, Keith managed a hard fought draw. Alas, for all our efforts, a 3-2 win for Macc C.

Another Momentum-building Win [Hat-man Rickie's account]

The Macc `C` Juggernaut roared into Cheadle last night, looking for a record fifth win on the bounce, and hoping to consolidate their position near the top of the table. Marc [aka Marc o'Polo] on top board was, for the second match in a row, in blistering form with the white pieces and a well prepared c4 opening opened up his opponent in quick time. 1-0 to Macc. [TR in quick time for Marc, but not for the unfortunate Paul the Dasher].

David S [aka David The Stylish] was next to finish and from the little I saw was in control for most of his match eventually prompting his opponent to resign. 2-0 to Macc

I was gifted a significant material advantage and immediately after this, my opponent left a knight hanging. Instead of closing out the game I succumbed to a mating net. Well played to my opponent and we'll move along (swiftly) 2-1.

[TR: Notice that Macclesfield's celebrity journalist, Hat Man Rickie, sensibly glossed over his loss which Edwin lavished so much space to reporting. whose epic will no doubt find itself reproduced in future chess anthologies if Edwin has anything to do with it].

Dave M [aka Dave Magnum Forced Draw] seemed to be treading a familiar path i.e. grabbing a couple of pawns and trading down. However, on this occasion, the wily Mr Vaughan planted 2 rooks on the seventh and forced a draw. 21/2 - 11/2

All eyes now on Board 4 where Tom [aka Tom 'Robbo' The Draw Bridge] was defending R + 5 pawns (1 passed) against R + N + 4 held by Keith The Draw Lion. Was my faux pas against Edwin the Fortunate going to be costly? A draw is offered, Keith refuses but then Tom wins a pawn (the only defence being a repetition) and with less time than Tom, Keith decides that discretion is the better part of valour and a draw is agreed.

3-2 to Macc `C` and another momentum-building win.

I Become a Registered Bunny

March 2016

March saw my nomination as a bunny rabbit, a weak victim to another player. Nemesis, who goes under the name Mike, was the instrument of my grief when I lost in four moves, in our last nightmare encounter.

From: Paul
To: all members

Stockport B 4.5 - 1.5 ECB

We were missing a few of our regulars on Tuesday night and realised we were going to be out-graded 30-40 points per board against a full strength Stockport B. However, we actually put up a really good show and were unlucky to get nothing out of the match at the end.

After losing in five moves last time against Mike, Tudor was confident of doing much better this time. He did. The blunder came on about move twelve this time (!) when, unfortunately, he overlooked Mike's bishop on b7 coupled with a queen raid along the g file gives a mate in one.

This is the sort of attack you learn as a junior but rarely have a chance to put into practice. Tudor rarely puts a foot wrong but has accepted that he is Mike's "bunny" now!

Bill was last to finish in an interesting unbalanced game. As per Bill:

He played an English Opening and we ended in a blocked position. He decided to unbalance and gave up a pawn and rook for two bishops.

He then decided to give up a P + R for 2 Bs. Only one of his Bs was active however, and were no open files. After I beat off his K side attack I countered and we were left to fight it out in an otherwise empty room. With five minutes on my clock and nine on his we agreed a draw.

I played against a *Benoni* type set up and was able to go two pawns up. I then played too slowly, and maybe too passive and reluctantly accepted a draw offer, as I was beginning to struggle on time a bit and conscious that I have been dropping pieces in time trouble recently!

Nick fought hard and applied some pressure but was unable to break through. It was a dead draw.

Edwin gets some great positions out of his queen's pawn openings and this was no exception. It was very even. He maybe should have exchanged queens when he had the chance, but in the end a sharp attack finished him off.

Dalai Lama Geoff, a willing recruit from the C team, played well against a *Queen's Pawn London System* and again it looked a very even game. Unfortunately, he fell into a discovered (or uncovered) attack and lost after that.

We will get our chance of revenge next Wednesday, when we host them back at our place

The A Team Roars Back

From: Phil
To: Club members

ECA 3.5 Denton A 2.5

Shortly after our recent victory against Denton, we hosted the rematch at home. Could we get a second victory and give ourselves a chance of staying up?

Steve played an aggressive *Dutch Defence*, throwing pawns forward towards his opponent's King and making him use a lot of time on the clock. Eventually an endgame was reached in which Steve had three pawns for a piece. A draw was agreed rather than play the time-trouble lottery.

John played a super sharp *Four Pawns Attack* against the *King's Indian*, gambitting a pawn to get one of his remaining pawns penetrating deep into enemy territory. He seemed to have to better of the complications, but his opponent fought tooth and nail and eventually John agreed a draw, rather than risk a worse result.

I was playing the same opponent as two weeks ago and with the same colours. I didn't want to just repeat the opening so instead played a *Modern Defence*, but wasn't totally familiar with the themes.

My opponent castled Queenside and threw his Kingside pawns at me. I responded rather slowly and although I eventually created some counter play, it was too little, too late and I got splattered. [Note to Caïssa - if one of my opponents could make a blunder this season, that would be helpful as I could really use a win!]

Geoff Bristle played solidly against another *Dutch Defence*, accepted a pawn sacrifice and consolidated his position. In the end his opponent blundered a piece as he sought complications.

Kieran got a nice solid position out of the opening but didn't find a way to seriously trouble his opponent.

Dave Dave's win was poetic justice for his defeat in the dying seconds of his game at Chorlton last season.

In Dave's words:

The final result will certainly not reflect the drama of my game. My opponent (graded only 117) played some odd looking knight moves in the opening but he may be related to Fritz *which pronounced that the moves were all sound.*

I pressed throughout the middle game, falling 20 mins behind on the clock eventually reaching an equal position. I remember looking at the clock and thinking that if only he had 5 mins left and I had 25 I might be able blitz him in the endgame, but of course in reality the 5 minutes were mine.

Then the fun really started. I was playing quickly and as often happens when one has a lot of time on the clock, he was playing slower and slower as we manoeuvred our bishops and kings around the board each trying to make something of a dead ending.

Eventually he offered a draw so I consulted Phil who said yes I could accept a draw. A quick glance at John's board suggested that was drawn and by now we were both down to two minutes. I still felt like I had some winning chances so I declined, and tried to apply more pressure. Eventually his flag fell (don't ask me what was happening on the board because I honestly couldn't tell you!).

Stephen thought I had lost on time (a perfectly reasonable assumption given my past history).

Kieran, with little filial loyalty, suggested in no uncertain terms that I was the luckiest man alive. As I pointed out to him "the more I practice the luckier I get!"

So another victory. If we can get something out of our matches against Chorlton, we have a chance of staying up!

[TR: Footnote

Ha! Phil's calm conceals the grim truth. The A team needs to get something out of a strong team to have a chance of staying up. As he noted earlier. This could get very interesting.]

May Caissa be with us

From: Tudor
To: All members

Some of us may have been puzzled about Captain Phil's reference to Caissa. (Unlike Phil, I can't do the funny dots over the i in Caissa).

I hastened to that modern plebeian spring, Wikipedia, to quench my curiosity. The following is based on what I found there.

Caissa, I learned, is the patron goddess of chess. Her rightful place came about after a poem in the classic style found favour among the educated class in London and Edinburgh.

Caïssa originated in a poem called Scacchia, Ludus which was published in 1527 and which describes in Virgilian hexameters a chess game between Apollo and Mercury in the presence of the other gods.

To keep faith with the classical style, the rooks are described as towers, (citadels in the corners, i.e. on their starting squares on the board) on elephants' backs, and the bishops as archers:

This led to the modern name Castle for the chess rook, and thus the term castling, and the modern shape of the European chess piece. For some time, some chess players in Europe called the rook an elephant and the bishop an archer.

Then the English Orientalist Sir William Jones re-used Vida's character in his own poem Caissa written again in Latin hexameters. with an English-language version for plebs (kind of him).

In this poem, Caissa initially repels the advances of the god of war, Mars. Spurned, Mars seeks the aid of the god of sport Euphron, brother of Venus, who creates the game of chess as a gift to help Mars to win Caissa's favour (all clear so far?).

Perhaps Phil was referring to Gary Kasparov's writings, where it is used as a substitute for being lucky with some move you can't work out clearly (Caissa was with me).

I am grateful to Phil for leading me to this wonderful poem. In that spirit, my wish, following Phil, for the rest of our season is 'may Caissa be with us').

I am copying this message to Syd, a classicist friend, for further insights, as my Virgilian hexameters have rusted through lack of use.

From: Tudor
To: Syd

Dear Syd,

I sent around the following message to members of my chess club. As my Greats mentor, and intellectual bodyguard, I thought you might find the contents of interest.

Some of us may have been puzzled about Captain Phil's recent reference to Caissa. I don't know if you have time to look at this.

From: Syd

To: Tudor

Will peruse this at greater leisure after the marking period. The English extract seems in general praise of Chess, and well written as such – hopefully his Latin is equally witty.

Have had time only for a quick skim look at the Scacchia poem. It's far more pretentious than the one from the English author.

It has chess invented for the recreation of the gods, and appears to describe an actual chess game, played between two of the gods on Olympus, as if it were episode of heroic warfare between characters e.g. a character/piece he calls the Bull, which may be a knight, charges enemy lines, and shortly afterwards dies in blood.

Very reminiscent of the power structure, heroic incidents and florid language of epic poetry like the Aeneid.

The board and the pieces are named and described in grandly emotional terms. I've no time yet to check the Latin in enough detail to see whether this is merely impressionistic movie-script heroics, or alternatively, contains enough technical information, buried within the florid Latin heroics, to enable the reconstruction of some actual game (if so, no doubt one with many dramatic twists).

If it is the latter, that may take some digging out, as it doesn't leap out at first glance.

Best regards
Syd

To: Syd
From: Tudor

This is no more than I expected of your scholarship, but wonderful to receive. My guess is that the elephants in the poem turned into castles in the future chess symbolism and design of sets.

Please continue after the marking marathon, although only if you derive some pleasure from it.

Warmest regards (diwlch)
Tudor

A Step Closer to Safety for ECB

From: Paul
To: Club members

ECB 4 - 2 Stockport B

Stockport B were looking to consolidate their position at the top of the table and put a strong team out. However, we had a few of our stars back and were able to avenge last week's defeat against them.

Dave Dave again played well above his grade. It wasn't all plain sailing against his strong opponent (the victor in Tudor's record four move loss) but Dave emerged a pawn up into the endgame, and kept it going for a fine win.

Keven played a *Catalan* and his light-squared fianchettoed bishop did the trick in neutralising the game for a valuable half point.

Dave the Power went a pawn up against heavy piece pressure on the open file on his flank. When the attack fizzled out, a draw was agreed with Dave facing a very active position and plenty of checks available to his opponent.

Another clash of the academics on board 4. Tudor may have been the bunny last week, but this week he was like a spring chicken! His focused and energetic display gave him a pawn advantage and he finished off Dr Baker with assurance in the endgame.

Bill allowed his opponent to get some open lines which allowed him to pick up a piece with a pin which had been overlooked by Bill.

I was a pawn up out of the opening but tried to simplify a little early and risked counter-attacks. Fortunately, it was still a complicated enough position and I was able to find a winning move.

So, all in all, a great result for us and it should be good enough to keep the B team in Division 2 for next season.

Footnote [TR].

Why am I less optimistic than Paul? I have lost too easily and too often from a winning position. Paul plays a bit like me, with few draws and more results that are wins or losses.

Dave the Power can be relied upon with his Fort Knox French. But he still likes to hold miser-tight to the half point he started the game with.

Dave Dave gets a good proportion of wins and only seems to lose if he is in time pressure. Unfortunately, he is often in time-pressure.

The exact survival task for will only become clearer as other results come in.

"Mr Baker, I Presume?"

Was there something structurally wrong at East Cheadle? The question was beginning to gnaw away at me. I began to re-examine the taken-for-granted beliefs held by most of the members, including myself.

When I tried to find answers from another chess-playing friend, her reply was quite instructive. I decided it was important enough to circulate to my East Cheadle colleagues:

From: Myself
To: All members

We make remarkable efforts to help everyone feel welcome at East Cheadle. Our distinguished President and committee members are particularly active in this respect.

However, when I approached Dr Baker, she wrote a lengthy and instructive reply. Her remarks about lady members and our loos are worth noting (my italics, not hers). I'm sure we will be able to draw this possible problem to the attention of the Memorial Hall committee.

From: Myself
To: Dr Jill Baker

Hi Jill
Hope all goes well Chez Baker,

I'm writing a *based on fact* story about a semi-mythical team in a semi-mythical league. In it, I muse about the failure of my club at East Cheadle to attract female members.

I wondered if you had any thoughts about the lack of female players in chess in general from your experiences. Is there some sort of discrimination at work?

From Dr Baker
To: Myself

Dear Tudor,

I wish you every success! Has the previous novel been published yet? [T.R. Yes it has.]

I often wonder about the lack of women in the chess leagues and I do not put it down to overt discrimination by the majority of chess players. In fact, I find it very refreshing that the majority of chess players do not even notice my gender. This includes the times when I've been very obviously pregnant (Once, when I was eight months pregnant, an opponent began the game checking he had my name right with "Mr Baker?").

There is some casual, unconscious discrimination and a lot of passive acceptance of this. The two on-going issues I have are around toilets, and males addressing groups of chess players assuming all-male gatherings. I do not play at one league club because the toilet arrangements are bad for men and terrible for women.

Your own club could also be a bit more thoughtful – the women's toilet is used by the men and the door does not lock (perhaps get the lock fixed?)

There is another club in the league where the path to the chess room sometimes leads past an exposed male bum, if a club member is using the very grotty loo next to the playing room.

It is commonplace for groups of chess players to be addressed as "gentlemen" at meetings irrespective of the actual composition of the group. This is hardly the most severe kind of discrimination, but it is quite hard to get the men even to acknowledge the issues. The lack of women means there's nobody to moan / laugh / take disruptive countermeasures with. If women were more numerous we would probably get the venues cleaned up or banned, issue a politely-worded requirement from the league to yourselves and others to do some minimal maintenance, and address chess meetings as "Ladies".

In the past, I've had worse. There was the occasion when two club colleagues insisted on accompanying me to an adjournment because they feared violence from my opponent (who didn't understand good bishop – bad bishop endings).

There has also been the infrequent unstable character I had to deal with when I was a league official.

But on the whole, chess is incredibly non-sexist. I've found myself in groups of teenage boys from Oldham discussing chess positions as equals, for example.

The worst ever chat-up line (30 years ago), incidentally, was "*you're the best-looking woman here*" at a chess congress where I was the only women aged between 12 and 60.

Really we have to look elsewhere for the issues, perhaps in schools for starters. For what it's worth, my own take on innate gender issues is that these are probably very minor rather than completely insignificant.

I'd love to be around when all the social stuff disappears, but I guess it will be centuries, not decades away. It wouldn't surprise me if women never number more than 20-30% of successful chess players, nor if men are only 20-30% of doctors. It's a subtle point lost on politicians that equality of opportunity will not necessarily lead to 50-50 mixtures, but is no less important for that.

The remarkable thing to me is that the evidence so far is that we don't have clear-cut gender differences so much as strongly overlapping populations.

At primary school level, chess is already private school and male dominated. Insofar as it exists in state schools, it is practised by boys and girls. At secondary school, it is uncool in state schools. Girls' private schools do not normally prioritise chess so it quickly becomes the domain of boys in private education.

So near and yet so far for the ECA team

From: Phil
To: all members

Chorlton 4: ECA 2

After winning two matches in row, could we get something out of our match at Chorlton, to climb out of bottom spot? With a couple of our top players away it would be tough, but miracles can happen!

Steve played his normal solid system against the *Sicilian* and swapped off into a slightly favourable endgame where he had the better pawn structure. However, there were no serious winning chances and a draw was soon agreed.

On board two I won. I had forgotten what that felt like.

My cause was aided by my opponent arriving quite late and then banging out several moves quicker than was necessary. We ended up in a another *Sicilian* [*Dragon variation*] but there was nowhere completely ideal for the White King. My pressure down the half-open c-file is thematic and told in the end. I managed to grab a couple of pawns and win the endgame.

Upon review afterwards the computer informed me that many of my moves were inferior but that is what computers are for!

Geoff grabbed a gambit pawn early on in a *Gruenfeld* and seemed to be a clear pawn up. However, he was always a couple of moves away from consolidating and his opponent played very enterprisingly, eventually pushing Geoff into a blunder.

Dave Dave seemed to get quite a lot of play in a *Dutch Defence,* but his opponent defended calmly. In time pressure (what else?) Dave was swindled.

Tudor went a pawn down early on in a *Queen's Gambit Accepted*, but had nice pressure in the centre to compensate. Sadly, Tudor's central threats did not come soon enough as his opponent's Queenside pawns were mobilised and the endgame was always going to be lost.

In a *Queen's Pawn* game, Bill played solidly and was content to gain a rapid half point.

So no miracle to report, but if we can get something out of our final match at home to Chorlton, we should still be safe.

"I might need some of your Players"

"I might need some of your players for the first team this week", Phil said.

"I was going to ask if you had anyone spare for the second team" Paul replied.

The captains of East Cheadle Chess Club A and B teams exchanged a look that said *we've been here too many times already.*

"We're in a relegation battle", Phil continued.

"So are we", Paul answered "John isn't back from France. Without him, it's already going to be tough for us."

Paul shook his head apologetically.

"I've got a vomiting flu victim available who said he would play if absolutely necessary. It's been going around. We could see if he would come in."

Phil winced.

"Maybe" he said, "we could see if we could borrow Myles from the third team. He is doing really well there."

If Big Sam can do it, so can we

The time for joking is over. We few, we happy few, we band of brothers have it all to do, as Big Sam put it.

For those unaware of his career, I should explain that Sam Allerdyce has been an English football battler, first as a player then a manager.

He has been accused of training players in the aimless long ball, hoofing up field. Sam observed that the criticism tended to come from managers of more glamorous teams he has beaten.

More informed football analysts think it is his attention to detail, careful preparation, and belief in solid defence, that have brought him success.

At the moment he is, like ourselves, facing a relegation battle with his latest club, Sunderland. A Houdini style escape act is needed if, you like.

When he was appointed its manager, at roughly the time we started our season in October, Sunderland was firmly rooted in the relegation zone of the Premiership. Sam coaxed, bullied, and dragged the team closer to safely. They now have a fighting chance to escape.

Going back to our own Houdini efforts, I know that at times I have lost games trying too hard to win. I fell into the Attacking Maniac style of play mentioned in the article I sent around. Now is no time for Attacking Maniac behaviour leading to losses.

Although it may be alien to my attacking style, I will do all I can to play taking care to keep a draw in hand. Then, if at any time there is a chance that a draw will set us on the way, I will accept one. Not only that, I will let the words escape from my reluctant curled lips, "would you like a draw?"

With such dedication, I belief that we will survive. If Big Sam can do it for Sunderland, so can we for East Cheadle.

With the benefit of hindsight, I can report that Big Sam succeeded in rescuing Sunderland from relegation yet again, and went on to become Manager of England's national team a few months later in 2016, after its dreadful showing in the European Cup.

Do not go Gentle into that, good Knight

From: Paul
To: Club members

Macclesfield B 4.5 - 1.5 ECB

As I abseiled the chimney-type access up to Macclesfield's new cavernous home in the sky, I was thinking this was going to be a tough battle for ECB against the league leaders. Indeed, that was to be the case, but as usual, we put up a good fight.

I didn't see anything of Nick's game, but he was the first to finish and set the night off well with a great win. Soon after, we were looking in good shape on all the boards with a possible upset on the cards. Then, soon after ten o'clock we ran out of steam and blunders took over for most of us.

The night marked the very welcome return to East Cheadle of yet another Dave. To avoid confusion with Dave the power, and Dave Dave, he has been temporarily designated Dave the Prodigal. He showed little signs of chess rustiness, and he played a really good game.

As per Dave the Prodigal:

The opening was the *French Winawer* variation which I like [TR: Dave the Prodigal was playing a *French Defence* in what was a close relation to the Fort Knox variation, but somewhat more counter-attacking]. Unfortunately, I met a line which I have not seen before. My typical game ensued – defensive and cramped.

I was twenty minutes down on time before I could play my counter-attack to free my position, and to start playing quick moves.

Within six moves, I had turned the game around, was level on time and it looked as though I may be winning. I could easily have asked for a draw but decided to push my advantage. I then miscalculated. Rather than consolidating for a drawn position, I tried a combination to win the exchange. There was a saving move which lost me a piece. Really enjoyable game as a comeback. All credit to my opponent for holding his nerve when the game switched around".

In my own game I started brightly, before being pegged back, but was ahead on time coming into a time scramble before (not for the first time) I inexplicably dropped a piece.

Tudor's sudden end was even less explicable. He had nearly twenty minutes left compared with his opponent's two and in complete control before he gave away a rook for nothing. Such a shame after a great show from Tudor.

New man Myles had come on board from the third team after great results there, unaffected by his leadership burdens. He was looking solid and came very close to having a draw offer accepted. The game continued though, and after play by Myles on the kingside had fizzled out, he fell prey to a deadly queen fork.

Or, as some players might have said, “I lost to that forking queen.” In chess, a fork is when a move results in an attack on two enemy pieces, and it is impossible to escape losing one of them.

After his recent warm weather training in the Canaries, David the Power showed no signs of running out of steam power. His top board game was the last to finish and he claimed a really good half point.

So, the result means we're not completely safe from the drop and our one remaining game against Denton B could turn into a crunch game.

Postscript [TR]

When Paul writes *Not completely safe* he reveals his customary positivity. His generosity about the increasing number of blunders I am making is saintly, or foolhardy. I restrain from weak excuses over eyesight, battle fatigue or age weariness.

I have petitioned him to be dropped further down the board order, which would be permitted to some extent, but I suspect Paul has a strategy to play to the strengths of his team, or maybe compensate for our weaknesses with who plays where and with what colour pieces.

After slightly the better start to the season, the B team now faces a struggle to escape from the drop, just as the A team does.

“You will be OK for seven thirty?”

I have finally arranged a meeting discuss removal of the cataract in my left eye. It turns out to be the afternoon of the last and vital match for East Cheadle B team in the evening.

I have timed the consultation expecting the operation to take place after the end of the chess season.

It has set me thinking about a bucket-list. That defiant term about facing mortality. On my bucket list: Visit Christchurch New Zealand again when there is no earthquake spoiling the experience; accept my partner Susan’s concerns that I am grossly negligent about my heath; play a decent forehand and astonish fellow members at the Northern Tennis Club in Didsbury; help East Cheadle avoid relegation

Then more introspection. Why I am so overweight that I am out of breath reaching rooms two flights of stairs above floor level for a chess match? Why am I increasingly clumsy, spilling food, dropping chess pieces in mid-move? Why is it hard to concentrate on what I am doing? Why am I so frightened of seeking medical advice?

It took far too long for me to accept that I needed eye surgery. It follows a pattern of procrastination most of my working life. I Never missed a scheduled lecture. Seeing a doctor could never be fitted it in during term time, and never during the conference season or brief holidays.

So, it's to be a late-afternoon eye examination tomorrow, giving me plenty of time for our home match in the evening.

I mentioned my appointment to Paul.

“You will be OK for seven thirty?” he asked nervously.

“We are minus our regular reserves”

If I didn't make it, the team would have to win on at least three boards. Our league survival depended on it.

“I'm no more than ten minutes away from East Cheadle” I told him confidently, “so I’ve plenty of time to get back.” Little did I think what was about to happen to me at the hospital.

Fifteen Minutes which changed my Life

However stupid my blunders in games, this has far worse consequences.

I am sitting in a crowded reception area at the hospital, waiting for a nurse to check my blood pressure. My consultation was set for four-thirty, but what that meant I was to arrive with the batch of patients then, and might be one of the last to be seen. It is now five thirty. I should still be in plenty of time for the match, although I will have to decide how to get something to eat before the game.

Quarter to six. Still half the people waiting. Too late to explain that I am in a hurry. A bad thought occurred to me, and my stomach tightened. The consultations should have been over by now. The surgeon was running late. I might not be out of here for another hour.

Six o clock. I change my mind, and head for the reception area to plead my case for being seen next. I start explaining my problem, when my name is called out.

I could still be out and at the club for seven thirty. Everything was going to work out nicely.

But the next fifteen minutes promised to change my plans not just for the evening but for the rest of my life.

“We'll keep you here overnight”

The distinguished ophthalmologist welcomed me warmly. He had performed the procedure for removing the cataract on my right eye three years earlier. I was convinced his surgical reputation was fully justified. He chatted urbanely as he completed the inspection and measurements, running through the risks (low) and benefits (high). My mind was partly on what opening I would play in less than an hour's time.

I had agreed the procedure should go ahead, and was about to leave, when the nightmare started.

“Just one more thing. I'd like someone take your blood pressure before you go.” I must confess that spooked me.

“How long...?” I began to ask

“The nurse will do it straight away.” Which I translated as meaning however long it takes.

I had been cornered. My blood pressure had been signalled as too high three years ago. I got away with a warning to see my GP, but the follow-up referral had never taken place.

Soon I was in a room with a friendly but no-nonsense Scottish nurse wielding a new-style stethoscope and the old style equipment involving a rubber band constriction device, arm for the use of. I found out is also known as a sphygmomanometer.

Six thirty. I could sense that any sphygmomanometric data obtained would be elevated by my general anxiety. “Always is” the nurse said “We take that into account.”

Six forty-five and I am back with the eye surgeon. I had put my overcoat on, and mentioned I had an important meeting starting soon. He looked slightly surprised.

“Meeting? Oh no, we'll keep you here tonight. Run a few more tests. Only a precaution. We can contact someone for you, about your meeting”.

For the first time, East Cheadle's Houdini needs were being replaced in my mind with a quite different set of worries. Just like that.

If this was in a chess game, I would say that I have reached a crisis moment. There is time pressure. The season-defining match is starting in less than an hour. The position is far from clear.

I run over the candidate moves rapidly.

1.1 I accept the offer to stay overnight. Which amounts to giving up and letting everyone down at East Cheadle.

2 I negotiate for my admission time to be put back to tomorrow

3 I make a break for it.

4.1 I say I need to secure my home, arrange for a neighbour to look after my (imaginary) dog

5.1 I make a hoax phone call to the police warning them of a device left at the Memorial Hall scheduled to go off at nine pm.

I tried option two with a dash of option four. "Of course. Would it be possible for me to get home first? It's quite close. I need to get a few things. I could be back in an hour".

My would-be medical life-saver-cum-gaoler remained inscrutable. Then he passed his judgement. "Go home? Not best. Hardly worth the disruption."

"I have a dog ..." I began. He looked pained, unwilling to enter negotiations. Then he spoke

"Dog? OK. I'll arrange an emergency appointment for you here tomorrow. Check at reception." I exited the consulting room, almost backwards and genuflecting. Thank you very much Mr Eye Surgeon.

A quick word at reception, and out to the car park. Where, in chess terms, I was hit by a bolt from the blue. I had parked in a prohibited space. A fluttering plastic bag on the windscreen told me I had violated the parking regulations. A yellow clamp on my rear wheel told me the nature of my punishment.

If my blood-pressure had been high enough before, I could feel it escalating. I seized the notice, and set off down the hospital drive, fumbling with my mobile to call a taxi. Why hadn't I put in the App my young nephew uses almost every day? My crap eyesight was kicking in. I couldn't remember how to Google for a number to call.

I wanted to avoid another visit to reception, where trouble is detected as if by trained trouble-sniffing dogs. I made my next move under extreme time trouble, and set of at a stumbling jog out of the hospital grounds for the road to Cheadle.

Houdini Time for ECB and Denton

From: Paul
To: All members

This was a big game for us. We needed at least a draw to guarantee we couldn't finish bottom. Denton is the only team that can finish below us. So it was a fight in which each club was battling against relegation.

As the time for the match approached, there were still players missing from both teams. Tudor had contacted me, and I knew he would be arriving. Even if late, he doesn't fall into time trouble.

I exchanged team order and names with my rival captain. The six boards were in place and ready for play. The clocks had been set for Fischer Time and double checked. [T.R.: Unintended pun.]

Roadworks around much of the Cheshire and Greater Manchester borders were making it a lottery who would arrive on time. Still no signs of Tudor, but even if he is late he doesn't get into time trouble. I was more worried about Dave Dave, who sometimes has as much time trouble arriving, as he does on the board.

Eventually we were mostly ready to go. Denton was still three players short. Then a break in our favour. Of the three, only one was making his way through the traffic. I expressed my condolences, all too aware that our task of surviving had been made considerably easier.

. Even more promising, Dave Dave arrives. It would be more so as long as Tudor is not much more delayed. Then the missing Denton player arrived, and we were almost ready to go. The clocks are started.

I could see one board at which the Denton player advancing a pawn, waiting for his missing opponent.

We still have a chance

A few minutes later and the hush in the room was broken as the door flings open. Tudor has arrived. But he seems in state of exhaustion as if he has been running in order to keep to his promise to arrive on time.

As he sits down, he dislodges the pieces at his board. But we still have a chance to avoid relegation. And we were already 2-0 up thanks to the Denton defaults. Dave Dave was looking good for a win on board one, and Fort Knox Dave was as secure as ever.

Tudor began playing even more rapidly than usual and his game had rapidly headed for an endgame with a slight edge for East Cheadle. Then his opponent offered him a draw, He consulted with me and I saw an opportunity to move the team to an almost guaranteed win.

Dave Dave was looking good for a win on board one. Why risk anything else? A draw was agreed on Tudor's board, one of the first he has obtained this season.

2.5 - 0.5 to us. One half point needed to escape relegation.

But then Dave Dave, without even being in time-trouble, made his move and realised he had chosen the wrong option. He lost the exchange, and then the position fell apart.

It was a shame, because without this oversight everything would have been wrapped up. Still, we only needed another draw from two games. But Jim was getting into a very complex position that could go either way.

At least we had our Fort Knox expert still at the board. Dave the Power even looks unbeatable, hunched over, leaning forward, moving swiftly and confidently. Who was winning? Perhaps his opponent, and anyway, he had to play on. Dave then exercised his draw-extracting process, honed by regular use. His first offer of a draw was declined. Then after each move or so, another offer, Dave gimlet-eyed, as if the draw was inevitable.

Eventually, it was too much to bear. Knowing the consequences, the Denton captain reluctantly yielded to the inevitable, and extended his hand, accepting the draw. We had escaped, perhaps not exactly in Houdini fashion.

Jim's game finished soon after. He managed to get his central pawns mobile which caused enough confusion to provoke a mistake from his opponent and gain Jim a well-deserved win. I was glad we had not had to watch that game end without the prior knowledge that we had saved ourselves from relegation.

So in the end, we won the match. Bizarrely, it means instead of ending up bottom of the league, we are now catapulted into third place, which is where we are likely to finish. Well done to everyone who has turned out for the B team this season!

[Postscript: T.R.]:

Fantastic. The B team is safe. But the A team still has to get a result. The consequences of a relegation by them would now be doubly bad, as we would find ourselves competing against each other, next season.

This drama is still not over. And I have to return, somewhat chastened, for my hospital appointment tomorrow morning.

"We Mean you no Harm"

I return guiltily to the hospital I had abandoned in haste the night before. I pick up a newspaper in the waiting room. Unsurprisingly, it is the Daily Mail of recent vintage. The main headline is something pithy about the cost to the National Health Service brought about by a swarm of illegal immigrants depriving tax-payers of its services.

I turn to the back of the paper for the sports. A photograph of someone in a hospital bed stares up at me. After a sudden illness during a training session, the England International cricketer James Taylor has been diagnosed with a serious heart condition. His photograph looks as if he has just been through the sort of ECG tests I originally ducked out of, and with which I am shortly about to be reacquainted.

He hit the sporting headlines a year ago, when he played a test winning innings, and took a miraculous catch. He was also dubbed the smallest man ever to play for England being closer to five than six feet in height. This adds to my admiration of him.

Taylor has discovered his cricket-playing days are over. Just like that. I was waiting for the tests which might have similarly life-changing consequences for me. It gave me time to think. About chess. About James Taylor. About me. I had no reason to suspect anything, but then, neither had James Taylor.

“Dr Tudor?”

A young nurse with reassuring smile appears, and I follow her into a little cubicle, not at all reassured. I assess her as a bit taller than the cricketer James Wilson, who is a bit taller than me.

It is a curious power differential as you strip to the waist, then lie on a couch as someone looking like an escape from a TV hospital drama appraises the landscape of your abdomen for the right places to attach a dozen electronic leaches. Should I say I'm not a proper medical doctor? Mention Tudor was my first name?

“Try to relax”. She has a relaxing kind of voice. It would work in a relaxation video. Or in a Sat Nav system: *You have just missed the roundabout for the hospital. Take the next left in two hundred yards.*

But how am I to relax here and now, staring at a bank of fluorescent lights on the ceiling? I wonder about that blood pressure reading which set of the chain of events ending with my arrival here. Had it been elevated to lights-out levels by tension too. It's a well-known example of the observer effect, and something to do with the ultimate uncertainties of the experienced universe.

I try to think relaxing images of a lonely beach, soft warm sand, a cooling breeze, creamy waves gently lapping against my bare feet. I still don’t feel relaxed. Something is wrong. “These two aren't working.”

Neither are my relaxation exercises. More sensors are gently reapplied to my chest and just above my multi-coloured socks covering my not bare feet.“Let's try again.” She sounds as if a lack of cooperation on the part of my newly-shaved epidermis is letting down the friendly little electronic workers deployed there. Eventually we are all ready for the measurement to begin.

"When I say, breathe in, breathe in and hold your breath until I say breathe out." It all could have been quite sensual under different circumstances.

Her electronic assistant joins in the conversation. It has a gently rumbling burr to its rather monotonous voice, which reminds me of the noise made by a central heating boiler. How long is all this taking? Bloody too long although I ignore the little voice of rationality saying it has been about ten minutes.

I breathe in and then out as requested, demonstrating my physical and cognitive alertness. Ominous silence as I continue to stare at the ceiling. Then I am gently uncoupled from the mini-Hal cum central heating boiler.

Should I plead for words of reassurance? Perhaps if she thinks I am a medical doctor she will report in the language one of her tribe, and not as to a captured alien being processed in a laboratory experiment ("We mean you no harm, strange little creature. Soon you will be released to go your way.")

It was too late for pleading. "We send the cardiologist's report to your GP. It usually takes two weeks."I can't detect good or bad news in the expression on the attractive young face that was looking down on me. I think I must have put my shirt and shoes back on, and exited stage-left clumsily through the curtains.

Can ECB win Three Matches on the Bounce?

From: Paul
To: all members

ECB 2 : Marple B 4

After 2 successive wins, we were faced with an under-strength Marple B, and had high hopes of making it three wins on the bounce. Unfortunately, Marple played much more strongly than their grades on all boards, and we got turned over.

Dave the Power seemed OK out of the opening but ended up losing a pawn and the exchange and the game.

Keven's drawn game became very tactical as he explains:

My game was a Philidor Defence. I got a lot of pressure but wasted a lot of time fantasizing about winning combos that each agonisingly had a single flaw. In the end, I opted to exchange down, but overlooked the loss of a central pawn.

However, I had sufficient play pressure to win it back and had marginally the better position but probably not enough to win.

Tudor was a pawn up but when the queens came off his opponent played a really good endgame and with opposite colour bishops, a draw was agreed.

As seemed to be the nature of the night, Bill was up against an inspired opponent who played well above his grade. In a *Sicilian*, it all started to get tactical and with pins on both sides it was Bill who came out the worse and donated a rook.

I played a quiet line of the *French* and whilst it gave me a solid position it didn't really give me much else.

Nick had active pieces and applied pressure but his opponent defended well. With only queens and pawns left, a draw was agreed.

So, too many draws and no wins for us on the night. We'll have another go next Tuesday, away at Stockport B.

This is it: Survival is getting tougher for the ECA team

From: Phil
To: all members

Our last match, against Chorlton, began with survival prospects for ECA team looking bleak.

The night got off to a strong start for us with super-sub Paul catching his opponent in a tactical trick and winning a piece early on. He then swapped off the pieces into a straightforward endgame. Well done Paul!

Tudor played an active *King's Indian* system and seemed to have good play against his opponent's king, but managed only a draw. It that stage there was still hope, as the other boards were looking good for us.

Geoff was playing his normal *Owen's Defence* and seemed to have an active position. He eventually won a pawn at the expense of a rather stranded knight. I was too busy with my own game and didn't see how this one ended. But then the news was passed to me to be recorded on the Captain's score card. It was a loss to us.

Steve was facing the *Alekhine's Defence* and had taken a risky pawn in the centre, leaving his Queen in the sights of his opponent's black square Bishop.

Then, after some complications, it became clear that Steve was no longer winning or even drawing. Eventually he lost the exchange and he had no respite after that. Another game loss for us. The match was suddenly getting unpleasantly close.

I was playing a *Sicilian Dragon* but had tried to avoid theory. An exciting game emerged, with kings on opposite sides of the board. Sadly, I was pushed into a position where I had nothing useful to do, while my opponent could attack my king at will. Eventually his attack stormed home. and I had to concede.

We had lost the match, as we had lost all three of our last fixtures. All our efforts to avoid relegation seem to be ending in desperately close failure.

Houdini Unchained

[Phil's report, continued]

Then the most remarkable twist to our season of twists and turns. Myles, who had been playing for the C team, had been checking the league website on his mobile for the latest results. What he discovered was to change everything.

I noted that he had been standing behind my opponent in some state of anxiety for some time. I thought it might signal his concern about my impending loss.

As I stood up to follow the remaining game, he whispered the news. A most favourable result for us had taken place, and had just appeared on the website. We both mentally recalculated what it meant. We agreed. Our fight was not quite over. We could afford to lose this match (we already had) but ECA might still avoid the drop from Division 1.

We were still a tantalising half a point away from avoiding definite relegation. But at least there was some hope. We both turned to the remaining game.

Who better to secure the half point than Dave the Power? As white, he was not playing his *Fort Knox* defence. His approach was as secure as ever. Could he complete our rescue attempt?

I guessed that his opponent knew how important a draw was for us, and that if he played on, then pressure, even on Dave's stubborn no-risk play, would grow.

Nor was the game completely straightforward. Either side could create more complications and increase changes of winning (and of course, losing).

Dave leaned forward, hand extended right across the chess board, and announced ‘draw’. His opponent looked around at his captain who seemed to be signalling that it was up to the player. His captain shook his head.

The game continued for a few moves. Now the other players whose games had finished gathered around.

Draw? Dave is asking again. If anything, he manages to make it sound that he was being insulted by someone who obviously had no idea of how to break through his defences. Elsewhere, tables and sets were being quietly packed away. The large clock on the wall was indicating we were heading for another late-night finish. Anyone who knows Dave will also know that extended matches do not bother him or shake his concentration in the slightest.

Another refusal. But the strength of Dave’s off-the-board play was getting to his opponent.

Chorlton’s captain, who was also the team’s car-driver, was playing nervously with his car-keys. This seemed to be the final signal for Dave’s opponent. He was the one who shrugged, offered his hand and accepted a draw.

There were no celebrations. The ECA team members looked disconsolate. Except for Myles and myself, they thought that the long season had ended in a position that even Houdini could not have scrambled free from.

As the visitors departed, I broke the good news to the dejected team members. There were rather weary expressions of delight.

Hardly the demonstrations at Leicester City, when its team avoided demotion from the Premiership at the end of the last season, and now were favourites for becoming champions.

But that's football, a different kind of beautiful game altogether. So, on that note, over and out from me after our miraculous Double Houdini escapes. Thanks again for all who took part in them.

PS: and look out for a new first-team captain next season. I am planning a much-needed sabbatical break.

One Small Move for Dave

The following message shows how close was the battle for survival by the ECB team. The author, Reg, pinpoints the game played by Dave of East Cheadle against his team the Altrincham Archers. He also sent me a file so that I could play the game through on a computer. This advanced civilisation technology will surely dominate over the efforts of romantics still playing chess as a congenial pastime. For the moment, one small move for Dave, one giant step for Cheadlekind,

From: Reg
To: Me

Tudor,

I've attached a document showing the end of the game with Dave, including comments. Also attached as a PGN file if you want to play through it on a computer.

The situation at the time was that the match was tied, with just this game left to finish. So quite a lot of tension, with both players short of time and a potential four-point swing in match points riding on the game. This proved crucial at the end of the season, as Altrincham finished bottom of the table, four points behind East Cheadle. Had I won this game, the teams would have finished level on both match and game points.

At move 31, playing as White I have extra pawns, but Black has compensation in a dangerous passed pawn and pressure on my position. I only have two minutes remaining on the clock, but Black is even worse off and is surviving on his 10 second Fischer increments. Then Black gives me chance, with a blunder which I could take advantage of, after the position changed and he misses the fact that the Queen no longer needs to defend, and I could move, take,

The game should now probably be a draw by perpetual, but for some bizarre reason I therefore decided that my Queen needed to be on a white square, and completely forgot that from my chosen white square it was not giving check, giving black a forced win, although in five straight forward forced moves. An interesting example of the silly decisions the human brain can make when under stress.

From: Tudor
To: Reg
Cc: Dave

Dear Reg,

Thank you for the fascinating game you sent me. We are at this moment investigating the claims of a miraculous Houdini act by Dave. You may know that two such acts are required before he is elevated to the position of Houdini master. Your own selfless gesture brings to mind the publication of 'The Immortal Game' between Kieseritzky against Anderssen. It was played in 1851 in coffee-house style at Simpsons on the Strand. On his return to Paris, Kieseritzky immediately published his loss in his own chess blog (sorry, I meant journal), so that the brilliance of the game should be remembered.

Who knows? One day 'The Immortal Game II' may be meet the same fate.

Man with the Hat

From: Tudor
To: All members

The season draws to a close. Our heroics will be remembered for as long as pawns are pushed at East Cheadle. In the midst of our celebrations I thought it would be interesting to share the reports from other teams.

Here is one from our near neighbours Macclesfield.

The club has been in trouble finding a regular venue. What follows is some extracts from their end-of-season report for their third team. Myles and his third team musketeers at East Cheadle engaged them valiantly and had two tough tussles with the champions elect.

Macclesfield's special correspondent, Man with a Hat, (Hat-Man Rickie, as Edwin had described him) has a sense of humour which is hyperbolic, sometimes confusing, and for me very funny.

I couldn't help noticing that Man with the Hat has the same problem as ourselves in distinguishing between a multiplicity of Daves in his team. Here are two more of his reports.

The Match that Won the Championship

Just a point required to be crowned champions. Still in search of a permanent venue, we entertain Altrincham in the basement of a community hall – with Zamba classes being held upstairs.

For those not familiar, the beat and more pertinently the loudness of Zanba is somewhere between the decibel levels at Notting Hill Carnival and that other one in Rio. Mercifully, the music stopped at 9pm.

Tom was first to finish with a win. Having struggled with his form in recent weeks, this was a gutsy performance to win when it mattered most. Next was Marc looking to avenge a defeat he suffered at the beginning of last month. Having engineered a passed pawn advantage, he was on top in a Queen & Double Rook ending when his opponent under pressure blundered and allowed Marc to fork his rooks.

On hearing the 2-0 score line, Dave M exchanged a solid and promising position for an agreed championship- achieving draw. Objective secured in an almost anti-climactic way.

David S, having fended off a vicious Kingside attack then went on to win his game meaning that the match had now been won.

The only blip was Man with the Hat's poor play, but full credit and congratulations to my opponent who did play well and thoroughly deserved his win.

There was still time for the championship winning captain to be carried shoulder high down to the Queens Hotel [TR: An appropriately named hotel for a chess club's celebrations] where a guard of honour had been formed to throw Man with Hat into a bath full of champagne after he nodded off, contented and with a glass of scotch in his hand.

A special thanks to Jenny for booking the venue at short notice and to the Altrincham team for being good sports when confronted with the cacophony which greeted them.

The Last 'Home Game' Played Away

Our last 'home' game of the season. Although officially a home game, this is now the fourth different venue for the last four home games and the Macclesfield Nomads are looking to make it an incredible nine victories in ten.

We start badly. First to finish was Mrs Hat. Regular readers of this blog will know that Mr Hat is neither brave nor stupid and does not comment further. 0-1.

Next, an almighty thud that triggered Tsunami alerts across the globe, as Marc throws down his King in disgust after ceding the advantage to a strong opponent. 0-2.

Dave M is having to play accurately to stay in this one as his opponent is peppering him with checks in a double Rook and Queen endgame but it's the Wilmslow player who makes the error and twenty minutes later its 1-2. Rook and opposite squared Bishops are a recipe for frustration in endgames. Then David S finished with aplomb. Well played Dave and David! 2-2.

Here we go again as the crowd tunes into another episode of 'An audience with the Hat'.

I now have not only a massive time advantage but an extra Bishop and only a passed pawn wedged into the 6th rank to worry about. I make this nervier than it should have been. When I finally wake up to the fact that I need to sac a pawn to create the play that will activate my pieces, my time advantage has been drastically reduced.

My opponent's clock however does run down, and although not the most satisfying of ways to win a game, a win is a win and this was my best of the season.

Altrincham Archers3 Nearly invincible Macc 2

More about Harry Houdini

As the season came to its dramatic end, I found time to find out a little more about Houdini. Harry Houdini was born Erich Weisz on March 24, 1874, in Budapest, Hungary. His family emigrated to America, settling in Appleton, Wisconsin, where he later claimed he was born. Fascinated with magic, he began performing and drew attention for his daring feats of escape. He changed his name in honour of the great French magician Robert Houdin.

Through the years, Houdini gained fame after repeatedly escaping from police handcuffs and jails. Harry was even given certificates from various wardens for escaping from their prisons.

After making his name in America, Harry toured Europe, where he expanded his repertoire by escaping from straitjackets and coffins. His exploits and photographs suggests someone who would have had a great impact on his audiences as a charismatic individual. Today, a hundred years after his exhibitions of escapology, his memory is still kept alive by references to a Houdini act facing an individual or a team. It was one such remark which resulted in the title of this book and the escape act which have I described in these pages.

By one of those coincidences which occur in real-life, I also described Sam Allerdyce's Houdini Act as being likely to save his football club Sunderland from relegation. Shortly afterwards, a local newspaper wrote an article under the title *The Houdini Act is Over: Have*

Sunderland found the Manager to end their annual tradition?

And that was exactly what happened. Except they started a new tradition of failing to rescue themselves from relegation.

That's real-life for you. I don't think I would have dreamed anything like that up, and added it to embellish the tale of the Double Houdini.

But Harry met his end in a suitably dramatic fashion. As I read the accounts, a chill settled over me that was not warmed by the late Spring sunshine outside my office.

Houdini's End

It had touch of Greek tragedy, a touch of irony. He created his image as a worker of miracles, someone possessed with miraculous powers.

One day, on October 22nd 1926, in Montreal, Canada, two students turned up and were admitted into Houdini's dressing room. They were not his enemies, but came from among the legions of his admirers

Is it true, they asked, that you can sustain a blow to the abdomen however hard it is delivered?

Pausing as he dressed for the next performance on his gruelling schedule, he confirmed it was true. He had trained to prepare his musculature for any sort of punch.

Would he demonstrate his powers? Yes, he would. But that day he had barely time to ready himself. He took several blows from one of his physically strong admirers. He managed to avoid the humiliation of crumpling in a heap, before they were ushered out, their faith in their hero reconfirmed.

Houdini had sustained serious intestinal injuries which developed into peritonitis. He died nine days later, on October 31st. His website pointed out that even the great Houdini could not escape the battle with mortality.

For whatever reason, the story stays with me like the scene from Bergmen's classic Swedish film, *The Seventh Seal*. In it, a young knight is confronted by the figure of death, and tries to trick death by playing a game of chess for his life.

Like Houdini, he loses, but not before death plays several sneaky moves. Maybe they were to sustain the false hopes of the Knight.

Such gloomy thoughts. Don't they always follow the joys of winning? Or this season at East Cheadle, the transient joys of not losing.

There is a sense that if tomorrow is another day, next season will be another struggle just like this one has turned out to be. Our first and second team captains Phil and Paul are resigning, as is our utterly dedicated Secretary Dave the Power. The Dalai Lama has said he intends to step down at the of the coming season. I wonder if the new president will acquire than honorific with the post.

My circumstances are providing me with countless opportunities for contributing to medical knowledge, and for turning down offers take up such duties. I have plausible reasons for turning a deaf ear to such requests.

Have I mentioned my deafness? I will spare the details beyond saying it happened of a river trip in the Florida everglades on a motorized barge, before the wearing of ear protectors became obligatory. I am intending to decline, and not accept any such gambit, beyond one counter-gambit of my own (More about which, later).

I have almost always found a way out of committing to offers of high office. It has been my own Houdini act. Earlier, it was because I had too many deadlines of my own, papers to complete, journals to edit, conferences to attend. Then it was a life-threatening illness. Now it's whatever the various medical tests will turn up.

For all these reasons, I am beginning to realize guiltily that I have been fooling myself, if not some of my closest friends, for years. I wrongly believed it was in the best interests of East Cheadle to protect the club from my undoubted world-class incompetence in organizational skills. The other possibility is that as the economists say I have become a habitual free-rider.

Next Wednesday, I have arranged to meet the Dalai Lama for the last club night before we close for the summer break. The club is searching for volunteers for long-serving officials seeking to stand down. This is when I am hoping to offer a proposal of my own.

A Sad Conclusion to the Season

Major Max died peacefully last week. The Dalai Lama's sad news below reveals a picture of the Major which is quite different to the impression sometimes left in his messages to the club of an old buffer railing against the advances of modern day technology

From: The President [via The Secretary]
To: All members

Some of you may not have learned that Major Max passed away last Tuesday. He appears to have sustained a heart attack during the night, while operating his Radio Transmission equipment.
He was discovered in the morning by his partner, whom he met quite recently on one of his regular visits to Burma to meet up with some of his military friends.
Major Max has been a loyal member of East Cheadle Chess Club for many years.
Younger members will be unaware of his background. Although I am honoured to be considered among his friends, and visited him regularly, he rarely spoke about his past. I knew he served with distinction the Royal Northumberland Fusiliers in one of its motor cycle battalions during the war.
When I first visited his home in nearby Woodford, some years ago, I was astonished to learn that his apparent

rejection of modern computers did not extend to radio transmission technology, with which he kept in touch with like-minded individuals all over the world. It seemed he also used it to play chess, using Morse code, often throughout the night, to the end of his life.

He was particularly upset but not surprised at the chess scandal recently when a competitor in a tournament was discovered to be using Morse code to cheat his way to success.

I will be posting information about funeral arrangements on the club notice board.

Our Last Club Night of the Season

The last club-night before the summer break. It was a subdued affair. The Dalai Lama pinned up on the notice board an announcement of a planned memorial service for Major Max. Attendance was down, even for an end of season club night. Next season, like the *Benoni*, promised to be the son of sorrows.

Phil had dropped by to arrange the hand-over of duties to the new first-team captain Dave Dave.

I was playing a friendly game with The Dalai Lama at another table, intending to discuss with him my proposal for offering my services to the club in an unexpected capacity. He was hardly attending to the game. We had even left the clock at its starting position, showing it was set for a fifteen minutes Fischer time game. The news of the Major's death had visibly upset him.

I was intending to leave after the game, having promised to collect a meal from the New Orchid House, a walk of a few minutes from the Memorial Hall.

There was a gentle tap at the door, as if someone did not want to risk disturbing the players inside. Phil and Dave Dave did not seem to have heard the noise. As it was my move, Geoff got up and wandered stiffly towards the door.

He returned escorting in a smartly-dressed young Chinese woman and a tiny figure who looked like a pre-school child. The Dalai Lama introduced the mother as Mrs Hsu, and her daughter as Anita.

Phil looked up briefly. Was he thinking the same as I was, that they were from the New Orchid House takeaway across the road?

It seemed not. Mrs Hsu had brought you young daughter to join the club. She was in the process of transferring to a nearby High School.

Both parents were studying for degrees at Manchester University, she in Business Studies, and he as an Engineer. Mrs Hsu said they would share the times they would bring Anita to the club.

Phil was staring at them again, but then he returned to his discussions with Dave Dave. After a little polite explaining, I was about to excuse myself, and the waif-like Anita slipped quietly into my place. My proposal could wait.

The Dalai Lama reset the pieces, and as white made a first move. Unlike the Dalai Lama. He would usually offer a guest white and the first move. He had forgotten about the clock again. Anita watched expressionlessly, and I paused to say a few words to her mother.

The solemn little figure continued to examine her opponent, without making a move. Then she looked at the clock, and back at the Dali Lama extending a hand about the size of one of Geoff's spectacle lenses.

After shaking hands, she did two things rapidly and confidently. She first started the clock, and pressed it again to indicate that Geoff should have done that after making his move.

Then swiftly she played the first move of the aggressive *Sicilian Defence*, one considered too complex for most members of the club to risk. This child had received a good chess education from somewhere.

Phil had been watching with increasing interest, and now he moved to Geoff's side of the board. When he showed what he had on his mobile phone, a smile lit up Anita's face.

It was a page from a chess magazine. *Taiwanese prodigy beats GM in Manchester simul* said the headline. And the photograph showed someone who was obviously Anita Hsu shaking hands with one of our regional Grand masters.

"A junior who can play on our top board" Phil said.

"Our second junior in two years" The Dalai Lama said, cheering up rapidly "and our first female member since the time of the Major. Perhaps next year …"

I had no doubt that our new young member would attract others to the club. I finished his sentence for him. "… we won't need to struggle for a Double Houdini, next season after all" I added.

I had forgotten to mention that I was prepared to put myself forward as honorary publicity officer to the club. I was looking forward to spreading the news about our newest and youngest member.

Perhaps, I thought, it would make a nice ending to a book.

Notes and References

This section is primarily for readers interested in the chess references found in the story of *The Double Houdini* and for researchers needing to know more about the literature sources referred to in the text.
[EC, or ECC: East Cheadle Chess Club]

Preface

That title has already been claimed:
https://www.kickstarter.com/projects/2103426234/chess-matters
Reality check for ECCC Second team:
https://books.google.co.uk/books?id=bCFBCwAAQBAJ&pg=PA158&lpg=PA158&dq=bite+on+granite+chess&source=bl&ots=evpiyVIG60&sig=ojozRE0E4lSVxhwT5PzRxKSJqC4&hl=en&sa=X&ved=0ahUKEwi-i-Xcm7vMAhUqLMAKHf8IA74Q6AEINzAD#v=onepage&q=bite%20on%20granite%20chess&f=false
Bite on granite:
A defensive set-up by black, with a fianchettoed bishop likely to frustrate the attack and encourage wild moves.

In Cold Blood

I postponed writing the hospital drama:
Postponed but not abandoned. A rather rebellious draft has been struggling to emerge for nearly ten years from my extensive sets of notes and drafts. Not so much writers' block, as saying goodbye to a midnight visitor I am reluctant to lose.

Relegation Battles are behind us

From the President's concluding remarks: The President is referred to throughout as The Dalai Lama Geoff, to avoid confusion with the recently arrived Geoff, installed as a first team top gun.

The Fixtures Meeting

Enter the author as participant observer, an accepted type of research practitioner in books on research methods.

See:

http://psc.dss.ucdavis.edu/sommerb/sommerdemo/observation/partic.htm

'The technique is used in many studies in Anthropology and Sociology. Often the researcher actually takes on the role being studied; for example, living in a commune, becoming a firefighter, enrolling in flight training school, working in a mental hospital (or passing as a patient), being a cocktail waitress, living among the mushroom hunters of the northwest, or joining a cult.'

The unreliable narrator: A character who tells the reader a story that cannot be taken at face value. This may be because character is insane, lying, or deluded, or for any number of other reasons.

See: http://www.nownovel.com/blog/unreliable-narrator/

Welcome to the First Division

David's "Fort Knox" Defence: You will find many references to Dave the Power's Fort Knox defence. It is a variation within the French Defence, [1 e4 e6], itself an ancient defence considered safe and offering chances of counter-attack. Within the French, the Fort Knox variation is even safer, more solid, and (eventually) offers chances not so much of counter-attacking, but of wearing down White into agreeing a draw.

Don't Do as I Do ...

Here's how to win the ending:

https://www.youtube.com/watch?v=3m2oNtgNGFw.

http://www.angelfire.com/journal2/chess/pawnchains.html

The President's Cup

Keven was first to finish: Keven, a former B-team captain, and difficult man to beat. Now offers assistance, but often has other evening mind-games as captain of a pub quiz team. His preference for that over chess is influenced by his enthusiasm for empirical research into real ale in the Stockport and Manchester hostelries.

Reality check for the Second team

computer analysis by Fritz: Fritz is one of the most popular chess engines, which are systems for analysing games, drawing on its programming and access to millions of games of chess games in its data base.

Our Hidden Strengths

You can breathe it in the air, as one management guru described it to me:

pass:http://www.theguardian.com/news/2004/mar/08/guardianobituaries.india

Herman Hesse mysticism which mutated into the servant leadership movement:

See: https://hbr.org/2001/09/we-dont-need-another-hero; https://www.uc.edu/content/dam/uc/honors/docs/Leadership%20Documents/Servant%20Leadership%20-%20Robert%20Greenleaf.pdf

Why I am not a Grandmaster

my triumph against the New Zealand master Bob Wade: He was playing thirty competitors in the Under 18s tournament simultaneously. Several went on to become strong masters themselves. I did not.

My Memorable Games by Bobby Fischer: Originally in the descriptive notation. See https://www.scribd.com/doc/154097736/Robert-Fischer-My-60-Memorable-Games

The Charnley Cup

The Charnley Cup is the most prestigious knock-out competition in the league: The introduction to this section is unattributed, and must be presumed to have been written by the author. His admitted role as reliable narrator suggests that readers must beware of assuming that the league is a disguised version of The Stockport and District League, and its prestigious knock-out competition known as the Charnley Cup.

Enter Houdini

It is often difficult to establish the authenticity of a historic event: Quite so. This story has the ring of belief about it. But is the author warning readers that all may not be as truthful as it seems?

Another Heavyweight comes to Town

Bobby Fischer played such a move: A famous incident known to any serious student of chess history. Fischer grabbed a pawn with his bishop leaving it open to a well-known trap behind enemy lines. Debate has waged whether Bobby had boobed or calculated many moves ahead and got it all abit wrong. Club players think carefully, remembering what happen to Fischer, before playing such a move.

Don’t Do as I Do

Presidents Cup: The Replay

the classical book "My System" by Nimzowich: If you are a serious chess-player and haven’t read this book, do so, immediately, do not pause to read on, however much you are enjoying this book which is less touched by the genius of the author.

http://www.goodreads.com/book/show/1430989.My_System.

If you are not a chess player, remember when you have played a hundred or so games in league and tournament play.
Paul's summary of a very bad night: Paul's report mentions players and openings that may need some further explanation. Bill was becoming a powerful asset in the engine-room of B-team matches. His Caro-Kann is not as popular as it once was, and is solid enough to meet the safety criteria of Dave the Power's defensive repertoire as an alternative to his Fort Knox defence.
Keven, the former B-team captain, is also a hard man to beat. His opponent's Queen's Indian defence is deceptively quiet, and at this level tends to be an invitation for a draw. Its main idea is to set up the bishop on the long diagonal, fianchettoed on the square b7, and then snipe at the centre from the flanks.
Nick is a great registered member to have as a reserve, often called in uncomplainingly for the toughest matches when stronger players are unavailable.
if I had engineered a fools' mate:
Famous for being the fastest way to be checkmated in Chess. White has to collude for black to achieve the win in two moves. Of more practical interest, there are traps based on fool's mate, which can win against the Dutch defence, and the Owen's defence (both favoured by some EC2 players). Note for chess players: No need to go beyond Wikipedia for an introduction to these wins, all in under ten moves. https://en.wikipedia.org/wiki/Fool's_mate
I played as black a line in the Alekhine which often crops up. White gets a slight edge but with lots of complications for black. I even wrote my score sheet down wrongly, obviously in some La la state of mind. The moves as played were

1 e4 Nf6 The defining move of the Alekhine defence
2 Nc3 Not usual but very safe for white. 2 ...d5
3 e5 The best play is now d4 when both knights are attacked. After which white takes black knight on f6, black take white knight on c3. 3 ...d4
For the fourth move, white decides to capture the black knight on f6 black decides to capture the white knight on c3. White has a choice of several moves but mostly takes black's knight slayer on c3, and black has to decide which way to capture white's slayer on f6 to keep material level. I had decided to take his knight-slaying pawn with my g pawn.
4 ef6 4... gf6
Bad bad bad. That should have been played on move 5. I had not taken his knight on c3. *I had played 4 dc3 in my head but not on the board*. The game is now lost against an opponent of even strength. Mine was considerably stronger than me. So I was left with a pawn to the good and a knight to the bad.
5 Kte4
Black resigns.
Reality testing
Not that: No laughing matter. The author is walking around scary possibilities which may explain his lapses of concentration and general increasingly evidence of deterioration of physical and mental faculties.

Chess blindness

I was at Cardiff Arms Park, playing for Wales: This is the spiritual home for Welsh rugby in its capital city, Cardiff. Now it rests almost literally in the shadows of the vast new Millennium Stadium.

Fate was Unkind

Pere et fils had expected their opponents to play the King's Indian: Kings Indian defence or KID. Popular among several

East Cheadle players, including Phil and the author. In some ways similar to the Queen's Indian defence (QID), with a bishop a key piece operating from the g7 square. Because the queen and king have different positions, movement and status, the defences play out differently. The KID is more attacking and direct storm on the castle king are always a possibility for black, but also for white.

Dave Dave Springs into Action

my grade dropped to 141: Lucky you. Other members of the ECB team are struggling to get their grade up to the 140s, which makes us eligible to more out of the weakest category in weekend quick-play tournaments

Another Way of Losing a Chess Game

in our bathyspheric journeys of decline:

Older readers as well as historians may recall the journeys to the ocean bed off the coast of Bermuda in the 1930s by the intrepid voyagers William Beebe and Otis Barton. Their Bathysphere was a diving bell of claustrophobia-inducing proportions.

https://sites.google.com/site/cwilliambeebe/Home/bathysphere

In my Dreams

Edmond Locart: Pioneer of forensic science and of the Locart Exchange principle.

ehttps://leaderswedeserve.wordpress.com/2016/05/03/locards-exchange-forensic-principle-every-contact-leaves-a-trace/

Locart's exchange principle:

http://www.forensichandbook.com/locards-exchange-principle/

the biblical reference to ben Oni: This was the name his mother liked for her son. For some reason, his father

preferred the name Benjamin. However, the Benoni lives on as a chess opening. In contrast, I don't think there is a *Benjamin* or a *Locart Exchange* variation.
http://www.forensichandbook.com/locards-exchange-principle/

I Investigate the Blunder

the first sports book I wrote was Tennis Matters:
https://www.amazon.co.uk/Tennis-Matters-Dr-Tudor-Rickards/dp/151699647X

A New Year Dawns

Geoff played a London system: A queen's pawn opening where white plays an early bishop move to f5. Positional game considered somewhat solid, but trappy for black, and unusual. White plays for central pressure. Ill -considered counter-attacks may weaken black.
http://en.chessbase.com/post/the-london-system-an-opening-for-you

Dave Dave played his normal Dutch Defence: Another counter attacking defence against white's queen pawn openings. Dave Dave likes so-called accelerated attacks as black where white has to be precise very early on.

The Dutch follows after 1...f5 or 1...e6 2...f5.

Not as popular as 1...d5, or 1...Nf6, followed by one of the Indian openings (Kings, Queens, Nimzo variants).

Dave the Power played his normal Reti: The first great so-called hyper-modern attack. Bit like the Indian defences for black, with slow build-up, and 'power at a distance' for Dave the Power from the bishop on b2.

I Found this Interesting

Here are the five styles, with hints on how to deal with them:
http://www.thechessworld.com/learn-chess/18-general-information/426-5-most-typical-types-of-chess-players-and-

how-to-play-against?utm_content=buffer6b543&utm_medium=social&utm_source=facebook.com&utm_campaign=buffer

Dave did not say what style he chose ('in less than five seconds'). Based on considerable circumstantial evidence, he has labelled himself a perfectionist, always getting into time-trouble.

Doing a Leicester

I had been tracking the decline in Jose Mourinho's fortunes as the season unfolded:

https://www.amazon.co.uk/dp/B01BOYZ3F2/ref=dp-kindle-redirect?_encoding=UTF8&btkr=1

You'll never win anything with kids:

http://www.skysports.com/football/news/11661/9930930/you-cant-win-anything-with-kids-premier-league-winners-rarely-feature-many-young-players

What Have they done to my Brain?

a 'Petrosian' or no mistake mode: Nicely selected reference. Tigran Petrosian, a former world champion, was a subtle player who preferred to find risk-free ways of grinding down his opponents. He was known as the iron Tigron.

See Gary Kasparov's pen-pictures of the world champions in https://www.amazon.co.uk/Life-Imitates-Chess-Gary-Kasparov/dp/0099489864

Troublesome Time Controls

These emails are about the merits of the Fischer method of setting the time which players have to play a game. In Fischer time, each player gets a time bonus for every move played. This is only possible when electronic clocks are used. Such clocks came to East Cheadle very late in the day.

I seem to be in a minority of players considering the Fischer method to be a penalty on players who manage time pressure well.

Mea Culpa

Bill is one of more sprightly new members, scarcely a year or so since he was exercising his skills in carving out a new life for patients who needed improvements to their tickers. (Rather poor pun and reference to heart surgery, to make a connection with his *whole hearted* support of the Fischer Time control, and its dominance over chess clock times.

Getting our Act Together

look for 'general themes': As well as 'forking problems' mentioned above, Steve referred to being *skewered*. In chess this happens when a piece is attacked but moving it loses to another piece when is then exposed. A nice example played by English GM Nigel Short can be found here. https://en.wikipedia.org/wiki/Skewer_%28chess%29#Example_from_game

Early Season High Spirits

Dave Dave is in particularly high spirits.

A Close Loss to Macclesfield by the A team

Geoff played his favourite Owen's Defence: As Phil put it 'A hypermodern fianchettoed queen's bishop giving tactical chances in the centre and king's side'.

Geoff gave a lecture to the club about the defence, with additional contributions from John and other club members.

The B Team's Breathtakingly Beautiful Breakthrough

now we have to keep up the momentum: i.e. in our case win another game, to make it two for the season.

Chess in a Cold Climate

I decided to offer an alternative account: Humour is some cold comfort against the buffetings of fate.

A Point, a Point, my Kingdom for a Point!

Steve played a King's Indian attack: This is like the KI defence, but as white. Playing a defence which works for Black can be effective in reverse. Another example of a defence turned into an attack when played by white is the English game (1 c4) which echoes the Sicilian defence (1 ... c5 which black plays after 1 e4).

The Ocular Proof

Eventually facing reality about my fading eyesight, I recall childhood memories.

The Apotheosis of St Stephen

the fifty move limit on hostilities: here's how it should be done. http://www.chess-insights.com/queen-vs-rook.html

Crying over Spilt Drink

mentally alert, even buzzily-wired: Although advertised on the bottle as *Powered by Glucose ...contains 17% glucose...it's for that moment when you need it most. When the energy and the good times flow.*

As a former researcher into carbohydrate chemistry, I know that its impact on my alertness may have something to do with a less-advertised ingredient, Caffeine, which as the label says *may have an adverse effect on activity and attention in children*.

Well I never. ECA Manage First Win of Season

Steve played a solid Ruy Lopez: One of the most ancient of openings, as a defence (e4 e5). That's it. Millions of games have thrown up innovations for centuries.

A recent one breathes life into an ancient variation. It is called the Berlin variation, has certain wall-link properties, and makes Dave the Power's Fort Knox variation of the French Defence look relatively frisky.

Another Weird Way of Losing

I thought I would get some practice in for the final matches of the season. I took part in a rapid-play one-day event in which I found another way of losing.

A Dentonite Explosion

Scandinavian defence: aka the *Center Counter Gambit*. 1 e4 ...1d5. Just the opening for players who want to get opponents out of book and into complications quickly. If you like the Alekhine defence (I do) you will probably like the Scandinavian defence.

Bill walked home: Quite a step. Maybe Paul is being ironic. Bill is a long-distance cycling enthusiast.

promoted a passed pawn: if you have been following, even as a non-player you will know this means a pawn that has been pushed up the board as far as it can go, and turns into a more powerful piece, usually a queen.

A passed pawn is one that has no enemy pawn on files on either side which could halt its advance by taking the ambitious little critter.

I become a Registered Bunny

A sad and painful story.

So Near and Yet so Far...

Geoff grabbed a gambit pawn early on in a Gruenfeld:

This a complex opening related to the other Indian defences, and leads to unclear positions.

https://www.chess.com/forum/view/chess-openings/why-is-the-gruenfeld-defense-not-more-popular

Sicilian Dragon defence: One of the great counter-attacking replies to 1e4, involving 1 ... c5. Dave Dave plays a particularly aggressive version of this dynamic opening. Phil is playing black, and the customary ('thematic') exchange of black's c pawn produces a 'half open' file.

If Big Sam can do it, so can we

managers of more glamorous teams he has beaten:
https://www.amazon.co.uk/dp/B012O0UUQW/ref=dp-kindle-redirect?_encoding=UTF8&btkr=1

Do not go gentle into that, Good Knight

The French Winawer. Yet another variation of the French. and A more attacking one than Fort Knox variation so beloved by Dave the Power.

Houdini Time

After this match I realised I had never offered a draw throughout the season, and this was one of the first offered me. This is possibly because I am often in poor positions, even if I luck out a win from time to time.

Can ECB win Three Matches on the Bounce?

"My game was a Philidor Defence...": Another ancient defence, found to give black too few attacking chances. May be not as bad as it seems, as modern computer analysis reveals hidden resources.

This is it: Survival may still be Possible for the ECA team

We had lost the match: As this is all 'based on a true story' there can be no happy ending. Unless of course ...

Houdini Unchained

Dave (the Power) leaned forward: The correct way to offer a draw is explained in the league handbook. You make a move, offer a draw and press the clock (when your opponent's clock is then started). The draw is on offer until the opponent agrees, or makes a move, or loses on time. It I very rare if these protocols are obeyed at our level of play, and draws are arrived at in various other ways.

PostScript

Harry Houdini was born Erich Weisz:
http://www.biography.com/people/harry-houdini-40056

escaping from straitjackets and coffins:
www.thegreatharryhoudini.com

Glossary

This light-hearted glossary of chess terms offers support to readers looking for a guide to the game's arcane vocabulary. It demonstrates the contributions from chess playing nations around the world over at least a thousand years.
I have added special NTBCW [Not To Be Confused With] notes, which are instructive nuggets of information.
The glossary will be found particularly useful for non-chess players who may be reading this book. I have drawn on reputable sources found in various chess reference books, as well as Wikipedia, that modern bluffers guide to everything,

Algebraic notation: The modern official way of recording the moves of a chess game. [NTBCW: those equations you had to do in Algebra in school]

Annotation: A description of a game, often made by the player explaining what happened, sometimes to suggest deep and profound trains of thought during a game.
[NTBCW: a member of a Celtic family owning the O'tation Arms, a hostelry to the south of the Irish town of Connaught]

Artificial castling: To exchange the positions of the king and rook other than by castling.
Also known as "Castling by hand". [NTBCW: anything to be found in *The Hand-Reared Boy*, by Brian Aldiss or *Portnoy's Complaint* by Philip Roth]

Back rank: The first rank on the board for each player, i.e. ranks 1 and 8 in algebraic notation. It can become vulnerable to sneak attacks producing checkmate [see below] if it is not protected carefully enough. [NTBCW: reply to 'you smell rank' by 'you smell rank, too']

Backward pawn: A pawn in a position where it has been left behind by other pawns of the same colour, is difficult to advance and is vulnerable to attack from hostile forces. [NTBCW: an intellectually-challenged minion]

Bad bishop: A bishop whose movement is restricted by 'friendly' pawns on its colour squares and so is not much bleeding use, especially against light-stepping knights in the end-game.

Bind: Where a player has got stuck having to defend without any useful moves. An extreme example of a cramped position. [NTBCW: constipation, although you might think of it as a sort of metaphoric constipation on the chess board]

Bishop pair: When a player has kept both bishops. The pair is powerful because of the way they move, one only on black squares and the other on white squares, always diagonally. [NTBCW: Any suggestion concerning the activities together of two Bishops off the chess board]

Blockade: Stopping dangerous advances by a pawn by sticking a piece on the square in front, thus blocking its path to glory.

Blunder: A horrible mistake which a player immediately knows he or she has lost or seriously screwed-up the game. Bit like the everyday use of the term.

Book: Special use in chess. *'According to book'* means 'according to received wisdom published in chess books and journals, or increasingly held in memory by chess data bases and programmes.

Both sides of the board: This refers to territory on the board shared out between the Queen and the King. Both queens start out on the right side of the board. The king starts next to her on the left side.

Bunny: Unpleasant term for a weak player who acts like a defenceless bunny when confronted by the hypnotic gaze of a predator. "Hello little bunny" one player would say softly to his victim, on seeing a weak opponent drawn against him for the next round in a tournament.

Candidate move: I like this term. In Chess tutors encourage you assess a range of possible moves before selecting one to consider more deeply. These are said to be candidate moves. [NTBCW: a politician who changes his address when standing for office]

Castle: Several meanings, so concentrate here or you might make a blunder later.
To castle is to shift the position of two pieces, the king and a rook *in a single move*. The move was an innovation to speed the game up (like tie breaks in tennis, and penalties in football). You must do it in a particular way for it to be legal.

For example, neither piece must have been moved during the game. There must be no square being crossed by the king that is under attack from an opposing piece.
There are two versions, depending whether it is the rook on the queen's side of the board or the one on the king's side. [NTBCW: In cricket, the expression 'the bowler castled the batsman' meaning the batsman missed the ball, and the stumps were scattered in a satisfying way for the bowler. The umpire also likes it, because the decision is obvious and the batsman is out]

Check: A very important term. A move that directly attacks the opponent's king. In bygone days the move was accompanied by a polite call such as 'check to your king'. This does not happen so much today and in fast-play chess there are penalties if the opponent doesn't notice and moves illegally leaving the king in check.
Old chess joke from a patzer (cv) attempting to win by perpetual check against a street hustler
Patzer: "I've run out of checks."
Street Hustler: "That's OK, I take credit cards."

Checkmate: The final move from which there is no escape. All moves are illegal. One of the pleasures of chess is to be able to announce checkmate before an opponent can resign.

Chessmen: A deceptive term, now politically incorrect which among other reasons ignores the gender of the queens, Also, it can confuse. Trouble is, the term may exclude the humble pawns. As in the question *how many pieces are left on the board?*

So for the pedantically-minded, the choice is the politically incorrect but unambiguous *chessmen*, or the politically correct but ambiguous *chess pieces*. The term *chess person* has not caught on, and is not likely to, IMHO.

Combination: A sequence of moves calculated or assessed to lead to an advantage. *'Combos'* often involve a sacrifice for other *compensation*, which we are about to come to.

Compensation: An advantage that offsets an advantage gained by the opponent, for example material vs. development, free movement versus a bind.

Cramped: Bit like a bind, but not quite as serious.
[NTBCW: dreadful leg pains though sitting too long in the same position, e.g. during a chess game. There have been reported case of chess players have had to be taken to hospital, after a cramped position resulted in a broken leg].

Decline: When offer a piece you can decline to take. In romantic chess, pieces were offered (sacrificed) in wild attacks. The attacker gets depressed when an opponent just ignores the offer, and may make even wilder moves to provoke more exciting play. [NTBCW: deterioration of health or assets].

Development: Important principle of moving your pieces into play in a harmonious way for increased attacking ability. This is also known as *coordinating your pieces*.
Beginners ignore this principle, but so do the greatest players, as that's the way things go sometimes. [NTBCW:non-

chess terms such as management development, professional development, or physical development.]

Draw: Important term. A game that ends with honours even. Sometimes a draw is forced, due to the rules of chess; sometimes by agreement. A weaker player may try to obtain a draw by making an offer, more in hope than anything else, because an opponent may have a host of reasons why he or she would rather be somewhere else. The stronger player will decline unless there is a serious chance of a loss which the opponent may eventually see. A friend of mine always leans forward confidently, as if he is doing his opponent a favour when offering a draw [Well, OK, he appears elsewhere in this book as Dave the Power].

Elo rating: You don't need to know how this works, but should know what it does. It calculates how strong you are from games you have played in official matches.
The system was created by Professor Arpad Elo. The Elo rating is the foundation for the award of FIDE titles.

Endgame: Obviously the period when the game is drawing to a close. Much mostly pointless argument occurs about when the endgame starts and the middle-game ends.

En passant: French *in passing*. Another innovation which followed from the earlier speed-up idea permitting pawns to take two steps forwards on their first move. Traditionalists fought and won the right to counter the move if in the older one-step at a time games the pawn could have been taken en passant. Happens to me about once every two or three seasons. You can only play *en passant* on the move *immediately* after the pawn has made the double advance.

En pris: This comes from the French verb *prendre*, to take. An *en prise* piece or pawn is one that is unprotected and exposed to being taken and gobbled up (*pret a manger*, so to speak).

Exchange: Another term with several uses. To exchange is to swop off one of your opponent's pieces for one of your own. A rook for a rook, a bishop for a bishop or a knight (being roughly equivalent for the social chess player.
Another meaning is about giving up the exchange which means a rook is exchanged for a bishop or knight. This might be because of oversight or blunder. Sometimes this is deliberate when a minor piece is believed to be able to do serious damage before the usually stronger rook can punch its weight.

Fianchetto: Italian "on the flank". A modernist set-up in which a bishop is as a long-distance sniper thus attacking from the back and flank.
My chess master taught me how to pronounce it, [*ffianketto,* in Welsh] but it doesn't crop up much outside chess. [NTBCW: a special cheese in TV cooking programmes found in the *quatro stagione* pizza, invented by Antonio Vivaldi]

FIDE: Federation Internationale des Echecs, the world governing body for chess. Founded in 1924. As with FIFA in football, FIDE has been not without its controversies which included a bizarre world championship match between Kasparov and Karpov in 1984. This ended in farce after 48

games, with echoes of the infamous Fischer v Spassky match of 1972.
I have nothing more useful or funny to say about FIDE.

Fool's mate: The fastest way to lose by being checkmated. It requires only two moves, but requires helpful suicide by a cooperative opponent.

Fork: Important term. A form of double attack. Often it is impossible to escape both attacks, so being forked is something to be avoided. Sometimes used in a punny way (as in, *I was in a right forking mess in that game*).

Gambit: A term widely and loosely used outside chess. In chess a sneaky offer of material, a kind of sacrifice that often turns out badly if you accept it. Another word borrowed from the Italian, translated loosely as being tripped up.

Good bishop: You can work this out from the meaning of a bad bishop.

Grandmaster [GM]: The highest title that a chess player can achieve (apart from World Champion, who is usually but not always the highest ranked GM). It is granted by FIDE (again). On their way, GMs have passed through ranks of Master and then International Master.

Grandmaster draw: An uninteresting draw of few moves. A sort of pseudo-battle between two players not inclined to fight. Boo. FIDE has tried various sticks and carrots, but chess players can be stubborn critters.

Illegal move: What you are prevented doing according to the laws of chess. Napoleon was said to make a lot of illegal moves, but for some reason no one pointed them out to him. In some contrast, Miranda in *The Tempest* gently pointed out to her squeeze Fernando that he had just played an illegal one.

Isolated pawn: A sad case. A pawn with no friendly pawns on either side. A bit of an embarrassment, as it is a nuisance to protect. Can become a bit of a goer in an endgame, however.

J'Adoube: Not just important but very important. In a game, if you touch a piece your next move has to involve moving that piece. A mistake and you can lose. I have, a few times, in many years of chess playing. It happens.
So you need some way of touching a piece if you don't want to move it. This is where you utter (or mutter) *J'adoube,* [French *"I adjust"*]. Useful if a piece has been accidently displaced to the edge of a square, for example. The term could be brought into wider use, for example if as a male, you are a bit forgetful when leaving the loo, and re-join company to a humorous chorus of *You've got a security breach at Los Pantalones.*

Liquidation: A series of piece swaps. Good play to take sting out of an attack. Usually misguided by a weaker player who is almost certainly taking the uncertainties out of the position, the best chance for survival for the relative bunny [see above] NTBCW: violent removal of a human in spy movies and perhaps real-life.

Mate: See "Checkmate".

Opening: Yes, you guessed it. The start of the game, the part increasingly played through memory, with knowledge of openings, rather than through calculation.

Openings: A specific sequence of moves which have been studied and published over time. Many players have favourite openings and play them obsessively.
There are over 1000 openings and many, many more variations. The names have a romantic sound to them, evoking great players, places and tournaments. I play the *Alekhine Defence* and The *King's Indian Defence* as black; the *Queen's Gambit* as White.

Opposite colour bishops: You might work this out from good and bad bishops. Where each side has only one bishop that travels on squares of a different colour from that of the enemy. This can give a side a dangerous advantage in the middle game, but is often drawn if the game reaches the end game. Sometimes one bishop gets too bad and can't defend threats on both sides of the board, and pawn does a sneaky runner].

Opposition: Important technical term. In an endgame, it sometimes turns out to be advantageous to the player *not* having to move. The opponent is said the have the opposition, as it mostly requires the positioning of two kings *opposing* each other across the board, head on head, or diagonally. [NTBCW: Political opposition, although may be worth remembering that letting your opponent move may be to your advantage.]

Passed pawn: A pawn that has advanced past any enemy pawn that could hinder or capture it. In other words, it is on an *open file*.

Patzer: A weak play prone to blunder. Possibly from German with more than a dash of New York Jewish. http://www.merriam-webster.com/dictionary/patzer See also, *Bunny*.

Perpetual check: Unremitting attack on a king, without either player making progress. This may result in a draw through the fifty move law of chess, or through both players getting fed up with the position and having something better to do.

Poisoned pawn: A pawn which, if captured, would cause serious disadvantage to the capturing side. In fact, an offer you should always refuse. [NTBCW: another cheesy plot-line in a spy thriller where a pawn is treated with a lethal dose of poison]

Prophylaxis: A strategy which anticipates an acts to prevents a dangerous plan by the opponent. [NTBCW: medical term for anticipatory treatment such as inoculation, birth control measures or tooth brushing. Maybe it's not so far away from the medical use of the term, come to think of it.

Promotion: When a pawn reaches the final rank, it magically becomes one of the other pieces. Almost always a queen, but sometimes 'under-promotion may be better. [NTBCW: rising up the ranks in a career; marketing efforts for a product or service.

Rank: A row of eight squares across the chessboard.

Rating: See *Elo rating.*
Repetition [or Draw by repetition]: A draw if the identical position on the board has been arrived at three times during the game.

Resign: The end. *Finito.* When a player sees the position is hopeless, and ends before getting checkmated. Classically by knocking your king over with grace, concealing your anger. With more practice you may choose to graduate to a graceful handshake and smile. But rehearse that smile in front of a mirror.

Romantic: An era when all players attacked and sacrificed like crazy. If a sacrifice was offered, it was considered cowardly not to accept it. A romantic player is one who enjoys attacking and sacrificing.

Rook: another name for the castle, which is the piece looking more like a castle than a large black bird.

Simplify: Exchanging pieces in order to reach a winning endgame, neutralize your enemy's attack, or clarify the position.

Simultaneous play: Exhibition stuff when a strong player contesting a number of weaker players at the same time. Great fun. [NTBCW: playing away, a euphemism for what The Sun newspaper says is the behaviour of love-rats]

Stalemate: A curious one. A position is which the player whose turn it is to move, is unable to do so legally. According to the rules this is a drawn game which annoys the person which the more powerful [pieces left. [NTBCW: a partner who has lost all earlier appeal]

Swindle: A trick overlooked by a player in a strong position reducing him an inferior position and a sense of being cheated.

Time pressure: With the arrival of chess clocks players have to make moves in a given period of time. [c.f. tennis, golf, and so on]. Often happens. Some players seem addicted to time pressure. Gives them a buzz.

Zugzwang: German "forced to move". Unfortunately, if it's your move you can't say *pass, durchgehen,* or *kontinuieren*. See *Opposition*.

Zwischenzug: German again. An *in-between* move. A *Zwischezug* move often refutes a combination and wins the game.

Quiz Time

Test your knowledge of what you have read in The Double Houdini with the following quizzes by selecting the most appropriate of the three options offered for each question.

Quiz 1

1 Where is the East Cheadle Chess Club located?

The Conservative Club, Cheadle
Church Road Memorial Hall, Cheadle
The Church Hall, Bridle Way, East Cheadle

2 Who mentioned Houdini first at East Cheadle?

Dave the Power, after the author escaped, Houdini-like, from a lost position
Paul, after a close win by the second team when Dave Dave had two seconds left on his clock
Paul, remembering Phil's success at a rapid-play game at the Ethiad football stadium.

3 How many games did the first team win in the first three months of the 2015-16 season?

One
Two
None

4. How many games did the second team win in the first three months of the 2015-16 season?

None
One
Two

5.What is Dave Dave's self-confessed weakness in his chess play?

He is addicted to getting into time trouble
He writes his scorecard down wrongly
He is addicted to exotic gambits

6. What is not one of the author's self-confessed weakness in his chess play?

A tendency to blunder in good positions
Unwillingness to play when Manchester United are home at Old Trafford
An attack at all times approach

7. Which of his favoured openings is viewed with suspicion by his teammates?
The Owen's defence
The Dutch defence
The Alekhine defence

8. What is Paul's leadership style noted for?

His unfailing optimism before and after matches
His consultation of the I Ching before cup games

His warm-up sessions with team members at home games

9. What is Dave the Power's favourite opening?

The Fort Knox defence
The King's Gambit
The Newell-Tranter stonewall opening

10. What do Dave Dave and Kieran have in common?

Not a lot, deriving from the fact that Dave Dave is Kieran's dad
Both are collectors of Star Wars models
A lot, deriving from the fact that Dave Dave is Kieran's dad

11. What heroic feat by Steve brought a round of applause from the spectators

Becoming the first ECA player to win away from home in the 2015-16 season
A draw by the 'fifty move without a piece taken' rule against a strong master-level young player
Appearing for a match in shorts after a game of tennis

12. How did the Ethiad football stadium not come into the story?

Keven agreed a draw in a good position at Denton, to watch the second half of a game in the bar
Paul played a much-admired game of rapid chess there
Dave Dave made a good joke about Manchester City losing a football game on time there

Quiz Two

Test your knowledge of chess terms with the following quiz, by selecting the most appropriate of the three options

1. Backward pawn:

A pawn left unprotected and is easy to attack from the front
An intellectually-challenged servant
Adult material watched in a mirror

2. Bind:

A boring position
A cramped position
German for 'would you like a drink'

3. Book:

Austrian Chess and Poker champion
Consolation prize won by author in Singapore
Received wisdom about an opening

4. Bunny:

Form of chess where bishops as well as knights can hop over squares
Derogatory term for a weak player
Cockney slang for unthinking play [bunny rabbit: habit]

5. Elo rating:

English Logic Rating (applied to moves by a computer programme)
European Long-Game Official rating
The foundation for the award of FIDE titles

6. Opposition:
Opening strategy of imitating your opponent's move
Advantage to you if your opponent has to move
Resources to combat an attack

7. Prophylaxis:
Term borrowed from a Greek Football formation
A strategy which anticipates a dangerous plan by the opponent
Medical term for using aspirin to prevent heart attacks

8. Promotion:
When a player moves from Master to Grandmaster
When a second team captain becomes the first team captain
When a pawn reaches the final rank, and turns into another piece

9. Stalemate:
A blunder leading to a simple mate
Trying to bore your opponent by playing very unexciting chess
When to move is a disadvantage

10. Isolated pawn:
A pawn with no pawns of the same colour on either side (file) of it
A pawn advanced too far to be protected

A pawn with no pieces defending it

Answers to Quiz One

1. Where is the East Cheadle Chess Club located?
Church Road Memorial Hall, Cheadle

2. Who mentioned Houdini first at East Cheadle?
Dave the Power, after the author escaped, Houdini-like, from a lost position

3. How many games did the first team win in the first three months of the 2015-16 season?
None

4. How many games did the second team win in the first three months of the 2015-16 season?
None

5.What is Dave Dave's self-confessed weakness in his chess play?
He is addicted to getting into time trouble

6. What is not one of the author's self-confessed weakness in his chess play?
Unwillingness to play when Manchester United are home at Old Trafford

7. Which of his favoured openings is viewed with suspicion by his teammates?
The Alekhine defence

8. What is Paul's leadership style noted for?
His unfailing optimism before and after matches

9. What is Dave the Power's favourite opening?
The Fort Knox defence

10. What do Dave Dave and Kieran have in common?
A lot, much deriving from the fact that Dave Dave is Kieran's dad

11. What heroic feat by Steve brought a round of applause from the spectators
A draw by the 'fifty move without a piece taken' rule against a strong master-level young player

12. How did the Ethiad football stadium not come into the story?
Keven agreed a draw in a good position at Denton, to watch the second half of a game in the bar

Answers to Quiz Two

1. Backward pawn:
A pawn left unprotected and is easy to attack from the front

2. Bind:
A cramped position

3. Book:
Received wisdom about an opening

4. Bunny:
Derogatory term for a weak player

5. Elo rating:
The foundation for the award of FIDE titles

6. Opposition:
Advantage to you if your opponent has to move

7. Prophylaxis:
A strategy which anticipates a plan by the opponent

8. Promotion:
When a pawn reaches the final rank, and becomes another piece

9. Stalemate:
When to move is a disadvantage

10. Isolated pawn:
A pawn with no pawns of the same colour on either side (file) of it

61935739R00132

Made in the USA
Charleston, SC
30 September 2016